FA[IR]
DEAL

Office of
Fair Trading

D1647237

£1.25
G₃

London: Her Majesty's Stationery Office

Contents

Getting a fair deal	3
The law of the land	5
Think before you buy	7
Your rights as a shopper	11
Buying away from shops	29
More things you should know when buying goods	39
Things you should know about services	49
How to complain if things go wrong	57
Going to court	63
Who can help?	67
Buying now, paying later	71
Keeping out of debt	87
Buying your home	97
Who cares?	103
Look out for labels	121
Consumer bodies	125
Useful publications	126

Getting a fair deal

Whether you buy a dozen eggs or a diamond, a mixer or a motorbike, you want value for money and you want things to work. Most of the millions of items that are bought every day don't cause any problems but things can go wrong and it is infuriating when the shopkeeper tells you there is nothing he can do, or you bought the item by post and have no idea what step to take next. Does a faulty kettle have to go back to the manufacturer for repair? Can a shop refuse to give refunds as a matter of policy? Can you change your mind about wanting something after you have bought it? Is the law different at 'sales' time? If you buy on credit, how can you be sure you are getting the best deal? What can you do if the shop says it is not responsible for what has gone wrong?

Then there are problems that can crop up when you pay for some kind of service. Is it just tough luck if your coat is lost at the dry cleaners or your boiler blows up soon after the engineer has called? What can you do if the builder leaves your roof in a worse state than he found it?

Shopping can be fun, but new selling methods can be bewildering. You don't have to leave home to spend money these days. A knock on the door can lead to your being the proud owner of a new brush – or thousands of pounds worth of double glazing you never even knew you wanted. TV and magazine advertisements carry tempting offers of goods which can be yours in return for your credit card number. And sooner or later you are certain to receive a phone call from somebody trying to convince you that you need a new kitchen or bathroom or both. What can you do if there is something wrong with goods you've bought like this?

If the very thought of this kind of problem makes you sweat, this book is intended for you. It pays to be a sensible shopper, whether you are setting out with your first-ever pocket money or are having to manage the family budget. Knowing your rights – and your duties – as a shopper can make you more confident when you buy something or when you need to complain.

This book, however, is not simply about your legal rights, important though they may be. It tells you about other measures designed to protect you, how to obtain the best credit facilities, how to make a complaint if things do go wrong and where to turn to for help and advice. In short, how to get a fair deal.

4

The law of the land

Before you read about your rights as a consumer, it is a good idea to know a little about the law in this country.

Criminal law discourages behaviour which can be harmful to the community as a whole – like theft and drunken driving – and, in the field of consumer protection, deliberate fraud, false descriptions and dangerous acts such as selling bad food or electrically unsafe goods. Offenders are prosecuted, either by Trading Standards (sometimes called Consumer Protection) or Environmental Health Officers or by the police. In Scotland prosecutions in consumer cases are almost always brought by procurators fiscal. The punishment may be a fine, imprisonment or both. In England, Wales and Scotland the courts can order compensation for those who have suffered personal injury, loss or damage as a result of someone's criminal activity. If you've bought faulty goods, however, your best hope of compensation lies with the civil law.

Civil law concerns your rights as an individual, and the rights of other members of the community. For example, when you buy goods from a shop, the sale is governed by the civil law of contract. If the goods are faulty and the shop refuses to put the matter right, you, the buyer, can choose to enforce your rights under civil law by suing in the courts.

Statutory law Both criminal and civil law can be statutory, that is, contained in acts of Parliament. For example, the Trade Descriptions Act (see page 41) is criminal law, while the Sale of Goods Act (see page 12) is civil law.

Many acts passed today give the Government powers to make rules when these are needed. Such rules are generally either 'orders' or 'regulations' (some are mentioned in this booklet).

Common law is law which is not contained in statutes, but has developed over the years from decisions made by judges in court cases.

There are some differences between the laws of England and Wales and those of Scotland and of Northern Ireland and these are noted in this booklet in the appropriate places.

Think before you buy

'It seemed a good idea at the time . . .'

How many times have you rushed into a shop and bought something – only to regret it when you got home? The new coat, shoes, furniture or washing machine seemed a good idea at the time but somehow less attractive later. Perhaps you were swayed by appearance. The vacuum cleaner was an unusual colour, perhaps, but so heavy you could hardly lift it. Maybe the chair looked rather trendy but it was desperately uncomfortable to sit in for more than five minutes. It certainly doesn't help to know you've only got yourself to blame.

Sometimes the shop will let you take the goods back and will give you a refund but if they do it's a matter of goodwill. In law you have no rights if you simply change your mind about something you have bought, unless it is faulty or was misdescribed. So if you are buying something important or expensive it pays to do some research and to decide what exactly you want.

For example, when you are buying a new cooker do not waste your money on an expensive model with lots of functions you will not use, if the cheaper model has everything you want. Why pay for something you don't need?

Before you embark on an important shopping trip bear these few points in mind:

☐ **Think about what you want and need. Decide what are the important features for you.** *For example*, if you are buying a new washing machine, would a half-load or rinse-and-hold function be useful? Do you need a very fast spin? Make a list of your requirements.

☐ **Decide how much you want to spend.**

☐ **Look at the copies of the Consumer Association's *Which?* magazine in your local library.** It tests a wide range of products and its reports highlight 'best buys' and features of merit.

☐ **Find out how easy it is to look after the item you are interested in and to get it repaired and serviced.**

- [ ] **Look for the symbols** which show a product has been tested for safety and quality.

- [ ] **Don't impulse buy.** You'll be left with something you don't really want.

- [ ] **Don't be rushed into buying.** If you're buying a large or expensive item, browse in a few shops and take the time to pick up any brochures. Ask friends or colleagues whether they have bought something similar.

- [ ] **Don't feel you have to buy something** just to please the shop assistant. If he has spent time explaining the item to you, don't feel guilty if you can't make up your mind there and then. Just say you would like to think it over.

- [ ] **Shop around and compare prices.** Look for interest-free credit deals. If you want to buy on credit read the chapter 'Buying now, paying later' on page 71.

- [ ] **Choose where you buy with care.** It is worth going to a shop which has a good reputation for quality and for dealing sympathetically with customers' complaints.

Some retailers belong to trade associations which have drawn up codes of practice with advice from the Office of Fair Trading. There are codes for furniture, shoes, electrical goods, cars and mail order for example. They cover things like the information you should be given, service and complaint handling.

Sale of Goods Act 1979

Getting your money back

Acceptance

Replacements or repairs

Credit notes

Receipts

'No refunds'

Guarantees

Secondhand goods

Sales

Trading stamps

Can your rights be taken away?

Manufacturer's liability

Deposits

Goods on order: *what should you pay?*

Goods on order: *how long should you wait?*

Delivery notes

Buying privately

Auctions

Your rights as a shopper

We buy millions of items each year, mostly without any problems. But occasionally something does go wrong and it's worthwhile knowing what your rights are in case you need to complain. Be prepared. **Don't get ripped off.**

Here are three typical shopping problems:

1. You've just bought a pair of shoes. After a week, the seams come apart and the heel on one shoe wobbles. You haven't treated them badly nor used them for rock climbing for which they clearly were not intended.
Can you insist on a pair to replace them?

2. You want a food processor. You choose one and ask the manager if it is powerful enough to knead bread dough. He assures you it is. But when you start to make your first loaf, the processor can't cope. The shop doesn't have another model of any use to you and offers a credit note. You, however, want your money back so you can buy elsewhere.
Have you the right to demand cash back?

3. You send for a blue blanket from a mail order company. It turns out to be pink even through the box is labelled 'blue'. You don't want the pink one (it doesn't match your colour scheme) nor do you want to pay for the return postage.
Can you claim for the postage at the same time as you ask for the correct blanket?

'What are my rights?'

Sale of Goods Act 1979

The answers are in the **Sale of Goods Act 1979** which covers all goods (including food) bought from a trader, whether from shops, street markets, doorstep salesmen, in sales, at parties in private homes, or by mail order. It doesn't make any difference whether the goods are paid for in cash or by credit. Once the seller has accepted your offer to buy, a legally enforceable contract has been made which gives both of you rights and obligations. It doesn't matter if nothing is written down. When you say or indicate 'I'd like to buy this, please' and he says 'certainly' or goes to wrap it up for you or simply takes your money, the contract is made.

The seller has three main duties to ensure:

1. that the goods are of 'merchantable quality'
'Merchantable quality' means that goods must be reasonably fit for their normal purpose, bearing in mind the price paid, the nature of the goods and how they were described. The new shoes in example 1 shouldn't fall apart after only a week's normal wear; and a new cassette recorder shouldn't tear up a brand new tape. If goods are very cheap, secondhand, labelled as 'seconds', or 'sale' items, you probably cannot expect top quality – but they must still be merchantable.

2. that the good are 'fit for any particular purpose' made known to the seller
If you ask for goods (like the food processor in example 2) to perform in a particular way, and the seller assures you that they will, he has broken his contract with you if they don't.

3. that the goods are 'as described'
Goods must be 'as described' – for example on the package, display sign or by the seller. The blanket in example 3 did not meet the description applied to it.

Getting your money back

If any of these obligations have not been met the seller has broken his contract with you and you may be entitled to your money back or compensation.

You should always complain to the seller, not to the manufacturer, since in law it is the seller who is responsible for the goods (but see page 46 for manufacturer's liability).

Legally, the shop should collect faulty goods. But unless the item is large, heavy or liable to damage if moved incorrectly, it is usually best to take it back yourself. That way you can discuss the problem face to face, and it is much quicker. Remember, it will help both you and the shop if you explain the problem in a calm and courteous way.

You may be able to get all your money back if the fault appeared in the goods very soon after you bought them. You cannot expect to have the full price refunded if you have used the goods for some time. Exactly what you are entitled to depends on how serious the fault is, whether you have legally accepted the goods, how much use you have had from the goods and how soon you tell the shop about the problem.

You have the right to include in your claim any additional expenses such as travel or return postage (see example 3, on page 12). If you have to hire similar goods while yours are out of action, you may be able to get compensation for this too.

You may be able to claim extra compensation if you suffer loss or personal injury because of faulty goods – for example, if a brand new iron correctly used ruins clothes or gives you a nasty shock. Even if you accepted a free repair to your iron you could still claim compensation for your damaged clothes.

Acceptance

It is a good idea to examine and try out anything you buy as soon as you can. Once you have legally 'accepted' goods which are faulty you lose your right to reject them. This means that you are no longer entitled to a full refund – you can only claim damages, normally the difference between the purchase price and the value of the goods in their faulty condition. 'Acceptance' is normally deemed to have happened when you have kept the goods beyond a reasonable time. The law does not lay down any fixed periods – what is reasonable will depend on the goods and the circumstances. But you would generally be expected to make it clear to the seller that you are rejecting the goods as soon as possible after purchase. If you delay – or if the fault is only discovered some time after you have started using them – it may be too late to reject them and get a refund. If you sign an 'acceptance note' (as distinct from a mere delivery note) this may also be treated as acceptance and you will only be able to claim damages if the goods are faulty.

You are not entitled to anything if you:

☐ examined the item when you bought it and should have seen the faults then;

☐ were told about any fault (*for example*, the goods were described as 'fire damaged');

☐ ignored the seller's skill or judgment as to the suitability of goods for any particular purpose you described to him (*for example*, he told you that the food processor you were buying wouldn't knead bread dough – as you wished);

☐ ignored the seller's claim that he wasn't expert enough to advise you correctly about your purchase (*for example*, he told you he didn't know whether the glue you were buying would stick metal to plastic);

☐ simply changed your mind about wanting the article. Some shops do refund money or give credit notes in these circumstances, but they do so for commercial goodwill and not because they have to. Such traders may insist on seeing a receipt. And they will not usually take back something you have damaged;

☐ received the goods as a present (the **buyer** must make any claim).

Replacements or repairs

Provided you have not 'accepted' the goods you are

not obliged to accept a repair or replacement instead of cash compensation. If, however, you choose to accept a replacement or repair write to the shop saying that you reserve your right under the Sale of Goods Act to reject the goods. You can then ask for a refund if you are not happy with the repair or further faults occur.

Credit notes

Instead of a refund the shop may offer a credit note in exchange for faulty goods. A credit note lets you buy goods to the same value in the same shop. You do not have to accept one, but if you do, you will not usually be able to exchange it for cash later on. So you may be stuck with it if you cannot find anything else that you like in the shop. They are sometimes valid for only a limited period.

Receipts

A trader doesn't have to give a receipt or check-out slip, but it is a good idea to ask for one. If a receipt is given, keep it for a while as it is an excellent proof of purchase if you have to complain about faulty goods. But do not be put off by signs such as 'No refunds without receipts', which imply that complaints won't be dealt with unless you produce a receipt. Such signs do not affect your legal rights, and are in fact prohibited. If you see one tell your local Trading Standards Officer.

'No refunds'

Don't be put off either by notices saying 'No money refunded', even for sale goods. Such notices are illegal and should be reported to the local Trading Standards Officer. A trader cannot wriggle out of his responsibility if he sells you faulty goods.

'I can't do anything . . . the guarantee has expired'

Yes, you can! Your rights are not affected when any guarantee runs out. Whether a guarantee is offered or not, it is always in addition to your legal rights under the Sale of Goods Act. If you see a statement in a manufacturer's guarantee, which implies that you have no rights against the seller – ignore it! It is illegal to include such a term and it doesn't mean anything. It is worthwhile accepting the extra benefits a manufacturer's guarantee offers. It may cover a major component of a TV set for up to five years, for example.

If the manufacturer asks you to complete and return a guarantee registration card, there is no harm in doing this. In theory, a manufacturer could refuse to honour

a guarantee if you did not return the card. In practice, he is unlikely to do so, especially if you have some proof of purchase, such as the receipt. Keep your receipt and your guarantee registration card together in a safe place in case you need to make a claim.

Read the small print. If a guarantee, or extended warranty, is being sold alongside the product, think whether the price justifies the benefits which are provided. Make sure you understand what is covered, and what is not.

Some guarantees expect you to pay the postage, transport or even labour charges involved in repairing or replacing faulty parts. Others are for such a short period they are hardly worth having. Some exclude the problems most likely to occur. If your guarantee contains terms like these, you would probably be better off claiming against the seller if the goods proved defective. Under the Sale of Goods Act the shop is responsible for the goods, even if you have signed a manufacturer's guarantee.

If the fault is fairly small, you may decide it is quicker and easier to claim under guarantee than to go back to the shop. If the problem is so serious that you want to reject the goods and get your money back, you should claim against the shop. Manufacturers usually undertake only to repair or replace goods, not to refund money.

Companies which provide services, such as woodworm and damp treatment specialists, also guarantee their work – sometimes for 20 years or more. This kind of guarantee may offer valuable extra benefits but don't place too much weight on it: the firm may have gone out of business long before the 20 years are up. In some cases, the terms of the guarantee are so restricted that it is of very little help to you.

Secondhand goods

'My secondhand cooker won't work and the shop where I bought it won't help'

When a trader sells something secondhand it will probably not be in perfect condition, but it is still covered by the Sale of Goods Act. A secondhand cooker may have lost some of its sparkle, but it should be of merchantable quality and fit for its purpose – capable of cooking meals.

Your right to compensation will depend on many factors, including the price paid, the age of the article, and how it was described.

For example, if you bought a reconditioned vacuum cleaner – said to be only three years old and in excellent condition – which didn't work when you got it home, you might be able to get full refund or the cost of the repairs needed.

As with new goods, you can't complain about defects that were pointed out to you or defects which you should have seen on goods you examined.

It is a good idea to have someone with you to note what is said by the seller about an expensive secondhand item. In the case of cars, it's best to arrange an independent technical inspection before you agree to buy.

See page 26 for your rights when buying goods privately.

Sales

'I bought an electric kettle in a sale but when I tried to use it the water wouldn't boil. The shop said they

didn't have to give me my money back because it was a sale item'

Not true! Many people don't realise that sale items are covered by all the rules in the Sale of Goods Act. Goods bought in a sale must be of merchantable quality and perform the tasks for which they were made.

1. You buy an electric kettle, reduced in price because of a dent in its lid. When you get it home it doesn't work because of an electrical fault. You are entitled to compensation (see page 13) because the kettle doesn't boil water as it is supposed to do, and you couldn't reasonably be expected to know about the electrical fault.

2. By contrast, if you buy a glass water jug described as a 'second' and later find a slight flaw in its decoration, you are not entitled to any compensation. You should have known it would have some defect and it is still of merchantable quality, bearing in mind its description and, probably, low price.

For more information on sales see page 40 ('Misleading prices').

Trading stamps

Goods given in exchange for stamps, tokens or coupons must also be of merchantable quality. If not, you are entitled to compensation. If the supplier agrees, you may prefer to accept a replacement or something of the same face value instead.

Can your rights be taken away?

The law says a shop cannot duck out of its responsibilities to you. The **Unfair Contract Terms Act 1977** (page 55) prohibits a shop from 'contracting out' of its obligations under the Sale of Goods Act. And an order made under the **Fair Trading Act 1973** prohibits the use of any statement in a contract, order form, invoice, or guarantee, which seems to take away your rights. The shop or manufacturer concerned could be prosecuted. If you see such a statement on a document you have received, either strike it out or ignore it. You should, however, draw it to the attention of the shop – it could be old stationery, and a genuine mistake. Tell the local Trading Standards Officer if you suspect a deliberate attempt to deny you your rights.

Under the Unfair Contract Terms Act a trader cannot disclaim responsibility for death or injury arising from his negligence.

Manufacturer's liability

Under the Sale of Goods Act the retailer who sold you the goods is responsible for compensating you if they are faulty. But manufacturers also have a duty to consumers to take reasonable care that their products are safe. (See page 46: 'Product liability'.)

Deposits

You may see something in a shop which you'd like to reserve until you have enough money to pay for it. So you put down a deposit. Or you order something not in stock (or to be made specially for you) and agree to pay part of the price in advance to show you intend to buy. Similarly, you may be asked for a deposit towards the materials and labour costs of a service to be done later, for example, re-roofing your house.

In all these cases you are making a binding contract with the trader, so that if later you change your mind about wanting the goods or service the trader can sue you for his losses. In the case of a shopkeeper this could be the full price of the goods if he could not sell them to another customer. In the case of a builder his losses would generally amount to loss of profit but he could also demand compensation for any materials bought that he could not use on another contract.

Goods on order: what should you pay?

Once a contract has been made and a price agreed, the trader cannot ask you to pay more later. If you are expected to meet any price rises which occur before the goods are delivered, the trader must make this clear when you place your order. Otherwise, you should have to pay only the price you saw when you placed your order. Make sure you know where you stand, preferably by getting the details in writing.

When you order from a catalogue or brochure which says something like 'subject to price fluctuations' or 'prices correct at time of going to print' you may be bound to pay the current price if you want to receive the goods. You will have to pay any increase in VAT unless the trader decides to absorb it in his profit or the contract specifically says that no alterations in VAT will be passed on.

Sometimes it is possible, and desirable, to negotiate a contract allowing you to cancel or alter arrangements in certain circumstances without financial loss (nobody would want the builder to plaster the walls of a home extension before the electrician had done the wiring). But make sure any special arrangement you agree with the trader is put in writing at the outset otherwise it may be hard to prove later.

Be careful when paying a deposit. If the circumstances seem a bit doubtful don't hand any money over. If the trader becomes insolvent or bankrupt you may well lose your money and have nothing to show for it.

Goods on order: how long should you wait?

Suppose you want something for a particular occasion (*for example*, a bride's dress) and the shop has to obtain the goods specially for you. You will probably want to give a date by which they must be supplied, making it clear that if the goods have not arrived by then, you will no longer want them. If the shop agrees to your conditions (which are best put in writing), it is legally bound to have the goods ready for you by that date. If it fails to do so, it has broken its contract with you. You have the right to cancel your order and ask for your money back. You may also sue for compensation if you were forced to spend more money as a result of not receiving the goods (*for example*, if you had to buy a bride's dress at the last moment).

Even if you don't agree a date with the trader, he still has to supply the goods within a 'reasonable' time. What is reasonable for certain kinds of goods may not be reasonable for others. A plastic pedal-bin 'ex stock' might arrive within a few days but a settee upholstered in a fabric of your own choice might take many weeks. If you think a reasonable time has passed and you have waited long enough, contact the shop and agree a final date for supply. State clearly (preferably in writing) that if the goods haven't come by that date you will cancel the order and want your money back. If, however, you do agree to wait the longer time, you cannot cancel in that period without breaking your side of the bargain; the shop could be entitled to keep any deposit paid and even sue you for more money.

A mail order trader must send you goods in
reasonable time. If he makes his own deliveries you
can agree a date by when you want the goods. If they
don't arrive on time you can refuse to accept them.
But a mail order firm often uses a carrier (the Post
Office, British Rail, or a van service). In this case the
firm must make reasonable arrangements on your
behalf – that is, choose an appropriate means of

carriage, pack the goods properly and deliver them to the carrier in a reasonable time. If there is a long delay, and you have evidence that the goods were actually sent by the mail order firm to the carrier, all you can do is complain to the carrier – but you should pursue matters with the mail order company as well. (See also page 110 for the extra protection which codes of practice give when buying by mail order.)

Delivery notes

Sometimes you are asked to sign for goods delivered to your door. It is reasonable for a company to expect proof of delivery. But sometimes you are asked to state that the goods are satisfactory without having a chance to see them. Signing a satisfaction note could prevent you seeking redress in court, if the goods turn out faulty. So simply write 'Goods not examined'. If a package is supposed to contain more than one item check that they have all been delivered.

Buying privately

'What if I buy from a friend?'

When you buy something privately, from a friend, neighbour or newspaper small ad you have fewer rights. The Sale of Goods Act says that goods bought privately merely have to match their descriptions: they do not have to be of 'merchantable quality' or 'fit for any particular purpose'. Your other rights will depend on what is said between you and the seller – that is, what you were told about the value of the goods and their condition. If they are faulty, you will probably have to rely on what was said or written for any remedy. For this reason it is a good idea to take along a friend who is knowledgeable about the particular item, or who could act as witness, when you buy something expensive. Some traders, operating from their homes, use the 'small ads' columns in newspapers to sell their goods. This is fine as long as they make it clear that they are traders. But some pose as private sellers – a practice that is illegal – partly because they want you to think you have fewer rights than you actually have, and partly because they want you to think that you are getting a better bargain by not buying from a dealer. If you buy something faulty in this way, and you suspect the seller is a trader in disguise, tell your local Trading Standards Officer. If the seller turns out to be a trader you can seek redress under the Sale of Goods Act.

Auctions

Traders cannot normally get out of their responsibility for ensuring that the goods they sell are of merchantable quality, as described and fit for any purpose demanded by the buyer. In a sale by auction, however, a seller can exclude this responsibility, although such an 'exclusion' can be challenged in the courts as being unreasonable in any particular case.

If you go to an auction, read any notices and catalogues carefully. They may give conditions of sale about such things as payment, deposits and removal of the goods. Look at the goods and the catalogue description of them before the sale to see if they are really what you want and are worth what you are prepared to pay. Bear in mind, the moment the auctioneer's hammer falls, the last bid is binding – and it could be yours!

Buying from a doorstep salesman

Buying by phone

Buying at parties

Buying by post

Buying from a catalogue

Buying from a book or record club

Buying from an advert

Unsolicited goods

Buying at one-day sales

Buying away from shops

Nowadays it's sometimes easier and more relaxing to shop in the comfort of your own home – buying by post from catalogues, magazines or ordering by phone. Doorstep salesmen, sales representatives at 'parties' in private homes, and other traders, are all bound by the Sale of Goods Act (see page 12). The great majority of such traders are reputable and fair, and many firms who sell their goods in your home have agreed to follow a code of practice (see page 107). Unfortunately there are some who play on people's emotions and gullibility and a few, regrettably, are rogues. 'Caveat emptor' ('let the buyer beware') is a particularly apt phrase when buying goods or services from some of these traders! Here are some points to watch.

Buying from a doorstep salesman

'Good evening, I'm doing some research . . .'

- [ ] Check he is who he says he is (reputable companies give their salesmen identity cards).

- [ ] If you're not interested in what is offered, say 'no thanks' and shut the door.

- [ ] Don't feel obliged to buy anything if you don't really want to.

- [ ] Be aware of ploys to encourage you to buy in haste such as 'sign tonight' discounts or warnings that prices will rise 'next week'. Don't be afraid to ask for time to think things over.

- [ ] Apart from minor purchases, find out what similar goods cost in the shops before agreeing to buy.

- [ ] Get estimates from other firms for house repairs or improvements. (Some of the worst instances of cheating have been by 'fly-by-night' tradesmen offering to resurface a path or repair the roof.)

- [ ] Never pay in full before receiving the goods or service. If you pay a deposit, insist on a receipt with the firm's name and address on it. Check they are who they say they are!

- [ ] Don't sign anything without reading it carefully first, and making sure you understand it fully.

- [ ] If you want to sign a contract, but only on the condition that the goods are delivered by a certain time, then make sure this is in writing. Salesmen are often paid on a commission basis, and can sometimes make rash promises.

- [ ] If you do buy, find out and keep the firm's name and address in case of problems later. (It isn't much use having rights against the seller if you can't find him!)

- [ ] Make sure you know the true cost involved when buying on credit and compare this with the cost of other types of credit. If you sign a credit agreement in your own home, you have five days in which you can change your mind and cancel.

You have the right to cancel contracts made during a doorstep visit even when no credit is involved. The regulations apply where a trader visits you without invitation or after making a phone call. You will have a seven day 'cooling-off' period for cash contracts over £35.

31

Some businesses that sell from door to door are members of the Direct Selling Association, a trade body which has issued a code of practice for its members to follow. This includes a 14-day cooling-off period. The address is on page 105.

Buying by phone

Phone sales are becoming increasingly common these days. Don't be alarmed if you are asked for by name on the phone. The caller may well have got your name from the phone book. But your name could also be on several lists available to sales organisations. If you are not interested just say 'no thanks' and put the phone down.

Reputable companies should:

■ say who they are, and why they are calling;

■ phone you before 9 pm;

■ ask if it is a convenient time;

■ **not** phone you at work.

If you're interested, give yourself time to think the matter over and perhaps compare prices. Don't give your credit or charge card number over the phone if you have any doubts about the caller or firm.

Buying at parties

This means you can buy in a comfortable, relaxed atmosphere with friends or neighbours, where the demonstrator has more time to discuss the goods than in a shop. Millions of pounds worth of goods (including plastic containers, cosmetics, jewellery and clothing) are sold each year at organised parties and coffee mornings in private homes.

- [ ] Don't feel obliged to buy things you don't really want, just to please the hostess or agent, or because you don't want to look mean.
- [ ] Don't pay until you receive the goods.
- [ ] Try to assess the goods being offered, and the prices charged, with similar goods you've seen in the shops.
- [ ] Find out whether you can return goods you've ordered if you don't like them when they arrive, or if clothes do not fit you.
- [ ] Be sure to note the name and address of the firm, and the agent, in case you need to complain or exchange the goods later.
- [ ] If you are the hostess, tell the guests what the party is for when you issue invitations.

Many businesses that sell goods at organised parties are members of the Direct Selling Association (address on page 107). DSA members offer a 14-day cooling-off period with full refunds.

Buying by post

Buying from home through mail order has many advantages if you find it difficult to get to the shops, or prefer choosing your goods in a more relaxed way.

> You have the same rights in law when you buy through mail order as when you buy from a shop.

Buying from a catalogue

If you buy from a catalogue published by one of the large mail order companies which belongs to the Mail Order Traders' Association you are protected by the MOTA code of practice (see page 110). Check that delivery costs are included in the overall price.

Buying from a book or record club

By joining a book or record club, you commit yourself to ordering a certain number of items over the year. If you join, read the terms and conditions carefully. You may be sent the 'choice of the month' unless you let the club know that you do not want it. You may cancel your membership once you have bought the agreed number of items, but not before. Read your cancellation rights carefully before joining.

Buying from an advert

Whether you're looking at an advert offering clothes, furniture or gifts read it carefully, so that you know exactly what you are ordering. Keep a copy of the advert, details of your order and how you paid and a note of the date on which you sent it. This information could be useful if there are problems. **Never send cash through the post.**

The Mail Order Protection Schemes (MOPS) and the British Code of Advertising Practice operated by the Advertising Standards Authority cover goods ordered from an advertisement (see page 111).

Unsolicited goods

If you are sent goods you did not ask for by a trader who is hoping to make a sale, and you do not want to buy them, you have two options. You can write to the

sender, giving your name and address and stating that the goods were 'unsolicited'. If he fails to collect them within 30 days, they become yours.
Alternatively, you can do nothing for six months. If they are not collected in that time, they are yours to use, sell or give away. In either case, you must keep the goods safe for the specified period and give the sender reasonable access to collect them.

Under the **Unsolicited Goods and Services Act 1971** a trader can be fined if he demands payment for goods he knows you have not ordered. If you receive a bill for unsolicited goods, take it to the local Trading Standards Officer. In Northern Ireland the Unsolicited Goods and Services (Northern Ireland) Order 1976 applies.

Buying at one-day sales

One-day sales held in halls or hotels sometimes seem to offer amazing bargains. Some local authorities have drawn up codes of practice in co-operation with local Chambers of Commerce and organisations which may hire out premises for one-day sales. These codes state that the trader must display his name and address on all advertising material and at the hall itself, and conduct the sale according to certain fair trading practices.

If you attend a one-day sale, keep the following points in mind:

☐ Sometimes the low-priced goods featured in the advertisements are never offered for sale.

☐ At some sales all sorts of unfair promotional gimmicks are used like giving away 'free' goods or refunds to 'planted' buyers to encourage genuine customers to expect similar treatment.

☐ Be suspicious if the seller won't let you examine the goods. (Some rogues display good quality articles but actually sell similar items of inferior quality – this is called 'switch-selling'.)

☐ If you do buy something, try to get a receipt, giving full details of the trader's name and address. But be warned that the name and address may be false if the seller is a rogue!

Shops don't have to sell

Price display

Misleading prices

Descriptions of goods and services

Misleading advertisements

Food

Food labelling

Safety

Product liability

More things you should know when buying goods

Shops don't have to sell

A trader doesn't have to sell you anything. For instance, he may not wish to disturb a window display; or he may have put too low a price on the ticket by mistake and prefer not to sell at all than to sell at that price (although the latter case could be an offence under the Trade Descriptions Act). It is up to the trader to either accept or refuse your offer to buy.

Price display

With a few exceptions (see below), a trader doesn't have to display prices for his goods.

Unless anything is said to the contrary, it is assumed that when you contract to buy goods, you are agreeing to pay the currently displayed price including Value Added Tax (VAT) if applicable. Traders may, if they wish, display a notice saying 'All prices are exclusive of VAT'. Prices for food and drink consumed on the premises must, however, be VAT-inclusive.

Under the **Prices Act 1974** shops must display the prices of all items of food and drink. Where they are sold by weight, as are meat and most (though not all) fruit and vegetables, the unit price (*for example* the price per lb) must be shown.

With food and drink consumed on the premises, the price must be displayed where consumers can make their choice. Pubs, cafés and restaurants must display a selection of prices for meals and drinks. Garages must display the price of petrol on the pump.

Although a trader doesn't have to sell you goods, he commits an offence under the **Trade Descriptions Act 1968** if he deliberately displays a lower price on something than the price he actually charges for it.

Misleading prices

'Special offers', 'fantastic bargains', 'prices slashed'

These are a few of the many slogans traders use to entice you into their shops, particularly at sales time. But are the goods they offer really such bargains? The law has a good deal to say about the way prices are displayed. The **Consumer Protection Act 1987** will make it a criminal offence for a trader to display misleading price indications about goods or services. There will also be an official code of practice to guide sellers on how to avoid misleading price indications. As a general principle, prices and price comparisons must be genuine. Shops will have to take particular care with marked-down prices and comparisons with 'recommended' prices. A trader will also commit an offence if he claims that his price is lower than some other 'price' which does not exist.

If you think that a price is misleading in any way, contact your local Trading Standards Department as soon as possible.

Descriptions of goods and services

The **Trade Descriptions Act 1968** makes it a criminal offence for a trader to say or write something that isn't true about the goods or services he is selling. This applies to many different kinds of description – what the goods are, who made them, how they work, and so on. If a car has 20,000 miles on the clock or a trader tells you 'This pan has a non-stick coating', these statements must be true. Similarly, if a photograph on the label of a packet of prawn curry shows lots of juicy prawns, the contents must live up to the description. In the case of textile products, special regulations ensure that the fibre content is marked on them. The Trade Descriptions Act also affects services (see page 54), but does not apply to property (*for example*, an estate agent's description of a house for sale).

The local Trading Standards Officer enforces the Trade Descriptions Act, which also gives him power to enter premises, inspect and seize goods. If you suspect the law is being broken you should let him know. He may decide to prosecute. If convicted, a trader can be fined or imprisoned. In England, Wales and Scotland the courts can award you compensation if you have suffered as a result of the offence. You may, of course, sue the trader yourself.

Misleading advertisements

If an advertisement seriously misleads (*for example*, by wrongly describing an item or service, or leaving out important facts) then it, too, is covered by the Trade Descriptions Act. If you see an advert like this, you should contact your local Trading Standards Officer.

But apart from these statutory provisions, there are standards of taste and truthfulness which advertisements should meet. These are laid down in the British Code of Advertising Practice (see page 105: 'Advertising'), which is administered by the

Advertising Standards Authority. You should contact the ASA if you see an advert that you think objectionable or misleading in a paper or magazine. Enclose a copy of the advert if you can, or say where and when it appeared. If the ASA upholds your complaint, it can ask the advertiser to modify or withdraw the offending advert.

If you want to complain about an advertisement on TV or local radio, contact the Independent Broadcasting Authority (IBA). (See address on page 105.)

Under the **Control of Misleading Advertisements Regulations 1988**, the Director General of Fair Trading has 'long-stop' powers to step in following a complaint, but **only** if the public interest requires that a misleading advert complained of should be stopped by a court injunction. His rôle is to support and reinforce existing controls – **not** to replace them. And, in any event, he has no powers over TV/radio or cable advertisements, or many of those dealing with investments (which are a matter for the Securities and Investments Board – see page 105 for address).

Most complaints remain a matter for your local Trading Standards Officer or the Advertising Standards Authority to look into.

Food

The law gives you valuable protection when you buy food. The **Food Act 1984** makes it a criminal offence to sell unfit food, or to describe food falsely, or to mislead people about its nature, substance, or quality, including the nutritional value. Regulations cover food hygiene whenever food is sold, manufactured, packed, processed or stored for sale. Under the **Food and Drugs (Control of Food Premises) Act 1976,** when someone has been convicted under the food hygiene regulations, the courts can close down his premises if they find they are insanitary and a danger to health. (There are equivalent provisions for Scotland and Northern Ireland.)

Food labelling

Regulations under the Food Act also state that food must be labelled clearly so you know what you are buying. Labels must include the name of the contents, a list of ingredients, in descending order of weight, the address of the labeller or packer, and any food additives used. The **Food Labelling Regulations 1984** of the European Community Food Labelling Directive, state that water used as an ingredient in food must be shown on the label in its place in the list of ingredients.

Labels must usually show the date by which food should be eaten. Most foods must have a 'Best before' date, or in the case of food lasting less than six weeks a 'Sell by' date. The label should also tell you how the food should be stored. (Foods not dated include fresh fruit and vegetables, bread, flour, sugar, deep frozen food and long life foods.) Local authorities (in Northern Ireland District Councils) are responsible for enforcing these regulations. Scotland is covered by the **Food and Drugs (Scotland) Act 1956** and Northern Ireland by the **Food and Drugs Act (Northern Ireland) 1958.**

Under the **Weights and Measures Act 1985** the quantity of the contents (by weight, volume or, in a few cases, number) must be marked on the container of most packaged grocery items and many other goods. Items such as meat, fish, cheese and sausages (frequently sold as pre-packs in self-service shops) must either have their weight marked on the package, or the weight must be made known before purchase. Not all pre-packed goods must be marked however: *for example,* everyone recognises a one-pint milk bottle. There are also exceptions in the case of small packets. The Act also makes it an offence to give short weight or inadequate quantity, and to mark goods with a wrong indication of their amount.

Most pre-packed goods (such as sugar, butter, tea, flour) must be sold in certain prescribed metric quantities – *for example,* flour can be sold only in quantities of 125, 250, 500 and 1,000g (or in multiples of 500g).

Since 1979 the 'average system' of quantity control for certain packaged goods has been in operation. Under this system responsibility for the contents of these packages has largely switched from the retailer to the packer, who must make them up so that the quantity on the container is within certain limits laid down in the legislation. Enforcement generally takes place on the packing line.

Packers, importers and traders who do not conform to the weights and measures laws can be prosecuted and fined.

Trading Standards Officers are responsible for enforcing the law and ensuring that weights, measures and scales are accurate. (In Northern Ireland, the Trading Standards Branch of the Department of Economic Development is the enforcement authority.)

Safety

The law recognises that what you buy should be safe. Under the **Consumer Protection Act 1987,** which extended and updated earlier consumer safety laws, it is a criminal offence for a trader to sell unsafe goods. Products must meet the general safety requirement. This means that goods must be reasonably safe, taking into account all the circumstances, including the way in which the goods were marketed, any instructions or warnings given with them, any existing safety standards and any reasonable means of making them safer if possible. Some goods have to comply with specific safety regulations.

Breach of the safety laws is a criminal offence.

There are a number of symbols which show that goods meet certain safety standards (see pages 121 to 123.)

Product liability

The Consumer Protection Act also makes manufacturers and importers liable for injury and damage caused wholly or partly by a defective product **made after 1 March 1988.** In the case of injury or death, anybody can claim – not just the purchaser. Anyone whose property is damaged by a defective product can also claim under this Act – but only if the damage exceeds £275. But seek advice if you have been harmed by a product. You will have to show that the product did have the defect that caused the damage, but you won't have to show negligence or fault on anyone's part. The manufacturer or the importer (or the supplier if neither can be identified) might well contest the case. They might, *for example,* try to show that you misused the product – but the burden of proof is on them.

A 'defective product' is one that does not provide the standard of safety you are entitled to expect, bearing in mind its use and age. But a manufacturer cannot be held responsible for something he could not have known about at the time the product was made, such as dangers revealed only by later research or experience.

These provisions add to your existing rights relating to defective goods – *for example,* your rights to claim a refund or damages from a retailer. In Northern Ireland, there are similar provisions under the **Consumer Protection (Northern Ireland) Order 1987.**

What is a service?

Supply of Goods and Services Act 1982

Estimates and quotations

Completion dates

Choosing a firm

Paying in advance

Trade Descriptions Act 1968

Unfair Contract Terms Act 1977

Things you should know about services

What is a service?

Hairdressers, tour operators, builders, solicitors and car mechanics all provide services. Sometimes this service does not involve the sale of goods at all. In this category are the services provided by doctors, banks and dry cleaners. In other cases the contract you make includes both a service and the supply of goods – for example car repairs and building work.

Supply of Goods and Services Act 1982

The Sale of Goods Act 1979 is concerned with the sale of **goods.** In the main the 1982 Act protects you when you make a contract for a **'pure'** service (*for example*, the dry cleaning of a suit) or a contract for both work and materials. When contractors – builders, car mechanics and electricians – supply some parts or materials in the course of their work, your contract with them is for 'work and materials'. The materials must be 'as described', 'of merchantable quality' and 'fit for their purpose'. You have the same rights as you would had you bought the materials yourself.

The Act also sets out the standard you should expect to receive from someone who does work or supplies a service whether with or without supplying materials.

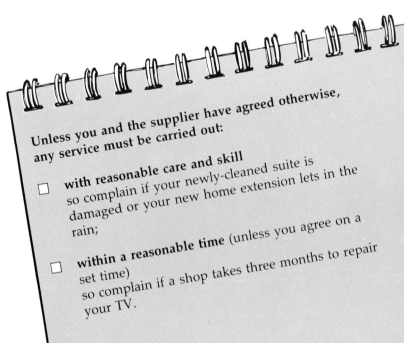

Unless you and the supplier have agreed otherwise, any service must be carried out:

☐ **with reasonable care and skill** so complain if your newly-cleaned suite is damaged or your new home extension lets in the rain;

☐ **within a reasonable time** (unless you agree on a set time) so complain if a shop takes three months to repair your TV.

You must be prepared to pay a reasonable charge
but you cannot complain later that a charge was
unreasonable if it was fixed at the outset, or some
other way of working out the charge was agreed.
So complain if a garage demands a sky-high payment
for a minor job. You can get an idea of what is
'reasonable' in your particular circumstances by asking
other traders in the area.

The part of this Act which deals with services does
not apply in Scotland but there are similar rights
under common law.

If you have problems with any goods supplied as part
of a service (windscreen wipers fitted by a garage) or
on hire (a carpet-cleaning machine) or in part
exchange (a new cooker for your old one), this Act
can also help you to sort them out.

Estimates and quotations

Always ask a trader to tell you how much he will
charge for a particular job. Decide beforehand
whether you will accept his good guess (what most
people think of as an 'estimate') or whether you want
a price which is legally binding (usually known as a
'quotation'). Whichever kind of price indication you
settle for, make sure you get it in writing, with all the
items listed. Find out if there is a charge for
doing this.

Because many repairs are hard to assess in advance
(particularly for cars and buildings), traders may be
reluctant to commit themselves to quoting a fixed
price. Instead, they prefer to quote a basic sum, and
add a statement to the effect that this doesn't include
anything else they might discover in the course of
their work. When you accept an estimate like this,
insist that the trader asks your permission to continue

with the work as soon as it becomes clear that his estimate is going to be significantly exceeded (he is, however, entitled to pass on any increase in VAT). Remember, you do not have to pay for work that you did not ask to be done.

Completion dates

It is sometimes important to have a job done by a certain date (*for example*, boots required in time for a walking holiday, or plumbing to be completed before the plasterer comes). If time is an essential part of the contract, agree this — in writing if possible — before work starts. Then if the firm lets you down you can cancel the contract and claim compensation for any loss you may have suffered.

Choosing a firm

It is always a good idea to ask for estimates from more than one trader. But don't automatically choose the trader who submits the lowest price. Try to settle on a trader whose work you have seen or who has been recommended by friends or neighbours. Quality is just as important as price.

Paying in advance

We're quite used to paying for goods and services in advance – at least in part – and receiving them later. It could be a fitted kitchen designed to your own requirements or double glazing and patio doors. But what happens if the company disappears or goes into liquidation?

Unfortunately there is very little you can do after the event. So avoid problems by following a few simple rules.

☐ **NEVER hand over money to a trader you know nothing about.** Sometimes it is reasonable for a firm to ask for a deposit to cover the cost of materials. Only pay if you are satisfied that the firm is reputable and an established business and that the advance is for materials. Don't pay the final bill until all the work has been carried out and you are completely satisfied.

☐ **Don't pay ANY money in advance unless you have to.** Sometimes this is unavoidable – if you are booking a package holiday or ordering made-to-measure curtains.

☐ **If you do have to pay in advance, either:** pay by credit card – if what you have ordered costs more than £100 and you have a problem with the trader, you may be able to claim your money back from the credit company;

OR, stick to companies belonging to trade associations that offer protection against lost deposits (called 'bonding' or 'indemnity' schemes).

☐ **If you pay by cash, insist on a receipt** showing the trader's full name and address.

Special points to think about –

■ Before you place your order check any special conditions. Could the price be increased before delivery or completion?

■ Do you need the goods by a certain date? If 'yes' – then say so in writing when you sign the contract.

Trade Descriptions Act 1968

Descriptions of services, just like descriptions of goods, must be accurate. If a sign promises '24-hour dry cleaning' or 'while-you-wait repairs' or a tour operator's brochure claims that a hotel is 'only half a mile from the beach' then the service should match the description.

The Act, as it refers to goods, is described on page 41. The same provisions apply to services, except that a trader commits an offence only if he knows the description of the service he is providing is wrong, or if he doesn't care whether it is true or not.

Unfair Contract Terms Act 1977

Some firms try to escape their responsibility by using 'exclusion clauses' or 'disclaimers' on their premises, tickets, contracts or booking forms – for example, 'Articles left at owner's risk', 'We take no responsibility for . . .', 'Departure times subject to variation without notice'. These statements try to limit the firm's responsibility for any loss you may suffer or for any damage to you or your property which occurs because of their negligence or failure to carry out their side of the contract properly. But they are not valid unless the firm can prove, in court, that the terms are fair and reasonable in the circumstances. And the notices cannot limit the firm's responsibility if personal injury or death is caused through the firm's negligence.

Four step-procedure
Step 1: *tell the seller*
Step 2: *seek advice*
Step 3: *contact a trade association*
Step 4: *further action*
Arbitration under codes of practice
Other special schemes

How to complain
if things go wrong

If you think you have a reasonable complaint about
something you have bought or a service that has been
performed, take it up with the seller (or, in the case of
a service, the contractor). You may dislike making a
fuss, but remember, if something is faulty and you
want the problem sorted out, you are not asking a
favour – you are claiming your rights. And
complaining can help achieve higher standards
for everyone.

Four-step procedure

If you think you have a genuine complaint follow this four-step procedure to get the matter put right.

Step 1 | tell the seller

Stop using the item and take it back to the shop (if you can) as soon as possible. Take a receipt or proof of purchase if you have one. (Remember, a trader cannot refuse to consider your complaint simply because you don't have a receipt.) Make sure you see a senior person: in a chain or supermarket ask for the manager. If your complaint is about a service, go back to the contractor, explain what is wrong and give him a chance to put the matter right.

If your problem is a tricky one it may be better to write to the firm's manager or managing director at the head office. To be on the safe side you should use recorded delivery. Keep copies of all letters. Do not enclose original receipts or other proof of purchase – just quote reference numbers or send photocopies. If you phone, ask the name of the person you're dealing with – you may need it later on. Afterwards jot down the date and time and what was said.

When you make your complaint, always stick to the facts and keep cool, calm and courteous!

If your complaint is about the unfit condition of food or food sold in dirty or unhygienic restaurants, cafés, shops, canteens, markets, stalls, delivery vehicles or suchlike, report the matter without delay to your local Environmental Health Officer (see page 69). If possible you should do this before you contact the seller.

Step 2 | seek advice

If complaining to the trader gets you nowhere, seek expert help and advice from a local consumer adviser at a Citizens Advice Bureau, Consumer Advice Centre, or Trading Standards or Consumer Protection Department. You can find their addresses in the phone book, or by asking at your local council headquarters or library.

The consumer adviser will ask you all the details and then may write or phone the trader to check the facts. Because someone else is taking an interest in the problem, the two sides can often reach agreement more easily, and the matter could end satisfactorily there. You can find out more about local consumer advisers and enforcement officers on page 68. Other sources of advice and help are on pages 103–118.

Step 3 | contact a trade association

If you are still not satisfied, find out whether the trader you're dealing with is covered by a code of practice (your consumer adviser may be able to tell you). If he is, either you or the consumer adviser can complain to the appropriate trade association (see pages 105–114). Most trade associations like your complaint to be in writing. Some provide a special form. The trade association's staff will then do all they can to try to settle the dispute.

Step 4 | further action

Sometimes – though not often – all this is not enough. If you are **still** not satisfied, talk to your consumer adviser. You could take the matter further by bringing a court case against the trader, or – in some cases – by using one of the special schemes that have been set up for resolving disputes between traders and consumers.

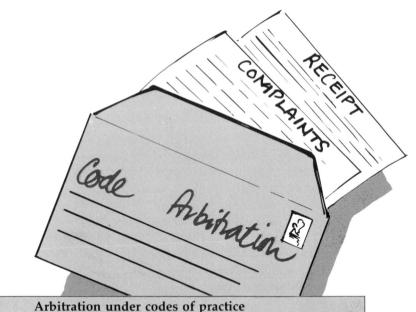

Arbitration under codes of practice

If the trader follows a code of practice with an arbitration scheme, you can ask for your case to be judged by an independent arbitrator (in Scotland an 'arbiter') whose final decision is binding on both you and the trader. In these cases the trader should not refuse to go to arbitration if you opt for it. But if you choose this method, you cannot later take your case to court, so decide carefully.

All the code of practice arbitration schemes (except for the Motor Code and Vehicle Builders and Repairers Code) are run by the Chartered Institute of Arbitrators. Code arbitration is intended to be a simple and inexpensive way of settling disputes, informally and as quickly as possible. It is based on a **documents only** system, which means an arbitrator decides the case on written evidence sent in by you and the trader. You don't even have to attend a hearing.

To apply for code arbitration, ask for an application form from the trade association, or from the Institute.

Other special schemes

Your consumer adviser can tell you if there is any other special scheme which you can use to resolve your dispute. *For example,* special arrangements exist for electricity, gas, telecommunications and other public utilities. Specialist schemes exist for dealing with complaints against solicitors and other professionals. Ombudsmen have been appointed to handle most insurance, banking and building society disputes and new arrangements exist for complaints involving investment and other financial services. See pages 112–118 for further details of some of these schemes.

County courts
Small claims
The Scottish system
In Northern Ireland

Going to court

County courts

Unfortunately, problems cannot always be solved on the trader's premises or by a consumer adviser. Sometimes it is necessary to sue the trader in court.

This need not be a daunting prospect because it is now much easier to bring small claims in the courts. The small claims system is designed to be used by private individuals, without the need to be represented by a lawyer. If you decide to take your case to court, discuss it with a consumer adviser first. An adviser can also help you to fill in details of your case on court application forms if you're the sort of person flustered by official documents.

If your claim is large or complex and you need a solicitor to represent you, the consumer adviser will help you find one and tell you about **Legal Aid**. This is a scheme, available to those of modest means whereby the Government pays all or part of the solicitor's bill.

In England and Wales the county courts deal with claims of up to £5,000. If you wish you can conduct your own case even if you have no legal knowledge and you will be given every opportunity to explain your case. If a large amount of money is at stake, however, it would be wise to consider being legally represented.

Small claims

If the sum you are claiming is not more than £500 your case will be regarded as a **small claim**, and will normally be settled by court arbitration. The small claims scheme is a quick and easy way of settling disputes.

If the sum claimed is higher than £500 and both parties agree, the registrar can order arbitration if this seems to be the best way of dealing with the case.

Cases heard by court arbitration are speedy, in private rather than in open court, and should be very informal. Lawyers are not often present and nobody wears wigs or gowns. The decision of the arbitrator carries just as much weight as a judgment given in court in public, but you cannot normally appeal against it.

Application forms are available from the county court office (the address is in the phone book under 'Courts'). You give brief details of the claim and there is a fee to pay, which depends on the size of your claim. Even if you lose you will not have to pay any legal costs (unless you used a lawyer yourself).

If you want to know more about going to law in England and Wales there are two booklets produced by the Lord Chancellor's Office which you can get free from the county courts or Citizens Advice Bureaux. They are **Small Claims in the County Court** and **Enforcing Money Judgments in the County Court.** Useful advice and information about the procedures can also be obtained from court staff.

The Scottish system

In **Scotland** there is at present no court arbitration system. There is, however, a **summary cause procedure** which is a low-cost way of dealing with claims of up to £1,000 in the sheriff courts. The leaflet describing this is called **Guide to the Summary Cause in the Sheriff Court.** It is available free from consumer advisers and sheriff courts. The sheriff clerk at the sheriff court, or one of his staff, will help you complete the form and tell you what fees must be paid. A new small claims scheme is shortly to be introduced. If you have a claim of £750 or less you will be able to take court action without using a solicitor, and the court hearings themselves will be more informal.

In Northern Ireland

In **Northern Ireland** the county courts deal with claims of up to £5,000. Informal arbitration for claims up to £500 is available. Ask your local consumer adviser, Trading Standards inspector, or court office (address in the phone book) for the leaflet **Small Claims Court**.

Trading Standards/
Consumer Protection Departments
Environmental Health Departments
Citizens Advice Bureaux

Who can help?

If you have a shopping problem which you cannot sort out yourself, you may find it useful to get advice. There are several agencies which can help. Most consumer legislation is enforced by the local authorities (except in Northern Ireland where different arrangements apply). Here is a guide to 'who does what'.

Trading Standards/Consumer Protection Departments

Trading Standards Officers investigate complaints and enforce laws relating to false or misleading descriptions of prices, inaccurate weights and measures and some aspects of the safety of goods. Often there will be a consumer credit specialist who enforces parts of the Consumer Credit Act. Responsibility for enforcing the law on some food matters, such as composition and labelling, also lies with them (but see 'Environmental Health Departments', page 69). If you are uncertain where to complain about any aspect of food and drink, first ask the Trading Standards Department. It will refer you to the correct department if it cannot help.

Your local Trading Standards Department is listed in the phone book in the section for your local Council. It may come under your County Council, Metropolitan Borough Council or London Borough Council. In Northern Ireland look under Department of Economic Development. In Scotland see the entry for your Regional or Island Council.

As suggested on page 58, try to sort out your complaint with the trader first. Trading Standards Officers are busy people and in some areas can help only if the law they enforce has been broken.

Consumer Advice Centres, are usually found close to main shopping areas. The staff, who normally come under the Trading Standards Department, give a wide range of information and advice to shoppers and traders, and deal with problems and complaints.

A few centres give pre-shopping advice as well. Mobile advice centres operate in a number of town and country areas. (In Northern Ireland, the Consumer Advice Centres are run by District Councils at Belfast, Londonderry and Newry.) They are listed in the phone book under Consumer Advice Centres, or in the section for your local Council.

Environmental Health Departments

They enforce certain laws that cover public health matters – for example, mouldy or contaminated food and drink and dirty places where food is stored, prepared, and sold.

Their work also covers cleanliness in other establishments used by consumers, such as hairdressing and beauty salons. In Northern Ireland, Environmental Health Officers deal with all food complaints, including those concerning composition and labelling and also with unsafe goods. In London boroughs, the division of responsibility between Environmental Health Departments and Trading Standards Departments varies.

They are listed in the phone book in the section for your local Council (in Northern Ireland under the District Council).

Citizens Advice Bureaux

There are about 1,000 of these up and down the country. They are independent and provide free, confidential help and advice.

Bureaux cover a much wider range of problems than just shopping: housing, employment, debt, marital and social security matters – in fact most things to do with day-to-day living. Some bureaux offer free legal advice, available by appointment only. Many will agree to act as 'go-between' in disputes between traders and consumers. Opening times of bureaux vary across the country, so it is a good idea to check before calling. They are listed in the phone book under 'Citizens Advice Bureau'.

What is credit?

Interest rates

How to compare credit offers

Types of credit

Bank overdraft

Bank ordinary loan

Bank personal loan

Budget account

Credit cards

Hire purchase

Credit sale

Credit unions

Finance company personal loan

Mail order credit

Moneylenders' loans

Mortgage lending

Pawnbroking

Trading checks

Hiring goods

Signing agreements

Keeping up the payments

Early settlement

Insurance for loans

Credit licences

Doorstep credit

Brokers' fees

Refused credit?

Equal liability

Extortionate credit

Buying now, paying later

What is credit?

You take out a mortgage on a house or raise a cash loan to pay for an unexpected repair to the roof; you buy a TV set on hire purchase or clothes on a budget account; you pay for a season ticket by credit card. In each case you are using credit. 'Buying now, paying later' is certainly convenient and very popular today.

It can make good financial sense too, provided you are sure that you can afford to keep up the repayments and that it would not be cheaper in the long run to draw on your savings.

Interest rates

Think carefully before buying anything on credit. Repayments almost always include a charge, normally called 'interest', for borrowing the money. Interest rates can be high, particularly in periods of high inflation. Sometimes there are additional costs such as administration fees or maintenanance charges, and the trader may calculate interest on these as well.

Interest rates can vary considerably. This is in part because some types of credit cost more to administer, or because the lender may charge more for a particular loan if he feels it carries a high risk. Interest rates may also vary between firms offering the same kind of credit – for example, the banks, finance companies, building societies or insurance companies which compete for your custom. It therefore pays to shop around for the best credit terms available to you.

Remember, too, that some credit agreements tie you to a particular maintenance contract for, say, a TV set. In such cases you might find it cheaper to look for alternative credit sources and make your own maintenance arrangements.

How to compare credit offers

Most loans to individuals for less than £15,000 (except for first mortgages with big institutions like banks, building societies, insurance companies and local authorities) come under the **Consumer Credit Act 1974.** The Act lays down rules about what credit information must be displayed on price cards in window displays, and all types of advertisements (including those on TV and radio). Rules also cover the way the information is displayed.

You should look for the following information in advertisements:

☐ The basic price of the goods or service – that is, the cash price.

☐ The rate of charge for the credit, or, as it is called, the **APR** – short for **Annual Percentage Rate**. This is the total cost of borrowing the money, worked out as a yearly percentage.

☐ The deposit.

☐ The period of the loan.

☐ The amount and frequency of payments, and what the whole credit deal will cost you.

☐ Whether or not you will have to offer any security for the loan. The 'security' could be your home, which you would lose if you could not keep up the repayments.

Because the APR must be worked out in a standard way and include all the charges you have to pay to obtain the credit, you can use it to compare one type of credit with another and one trader's terms with another. Generally, the lower the APR, the better the credit deal.

If there is any information you need which is not contained in an advertisment offering credit, ask for a written quotation. This must give the APR and all other relevant details. You can ask for written quotations from several traders and choose the best deal. And don't forget, when you are buying from retailers, you are not obliged to use the credit facilities they offer – you may be able to find a better credit deal elsewhere, for example, a personal loan from a bank.

A price card, window display, or other advertisment can only claim to offer 'interest free' credit if all the repayments add up to no more than the price you would have paid if you had paid cash. It cannot claim to offer 'cheaper' or 'easier' credit than anyone else, unless it shows figures to prove it.

Types of credit

Listed below are some of the more popular types of credit.

Bank overdraft – you get permission to overdraw on your account up to an agreed amount and for a certain period. As you pay money into your account so the loan is repaid. Interest on the amount remaining 'in the red' is variable and calculated on a day-to-day basis. The manager may charge a fee for a large overdraft and ask for security, such as your house or an insurance policy (see 'Mortgage lending'). He can insist on repayment in full at any time.

Bank ordinary loan – available to bank customers only and usually for large amounts for a particular purpose approved by the manager. You agree with him the time you'll take to repay the loan and he may ask you to provide security (see 'Mortgage lending'). Variable interest is charged and usually at a rate slightly higher than an overdraft.

Bank personal loan – available to anyone, though security may be requested from a non-customer. There is usually up to three years for repayments, but more for certain purposes such as home improvements. Interest is at a fixed rate.

Budget account – offered by many stores, allows you to spend up to a certain limit, for example, 15 times the £20 you decide you can afford to pay in each month: you may spend up to £300, but must never owe more than this. As you pay back, so you can buy something else, provided you stay within your limit. Interest (often called a 'service charge' or 'surcharge') is charged on what you owe at the end of a specified period (usually a month). Banks also operate budget accounts which are useful for spreading the repayments of your regular bills.

Credit cards – issued by a bank or other finance company allow you to pay for goods or services wherever the cards are accepted, including abroad. You are given a 'credit limit' which means you may have up to that amount outstanding at any one time.

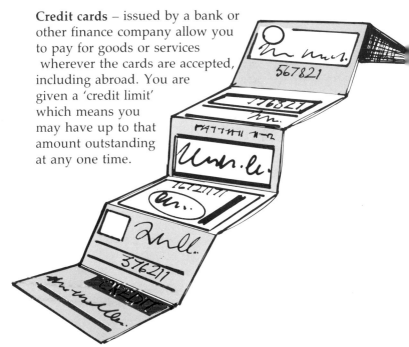

A monthly statement shows all the transactions you have made and the amount you owe, including any credit charge. There are two main types of card – a charge card and a credit card. With charge cards you usually have to repay the whole sum outstanding at the end of the month, so you only get a few weeks' credit. (Instead of interest they charge you an annual membership fee.) With credit cards you can pay back a small minimum amount, or more if you wish. If you pay up in full each month, you will not be charged any interest. (Note that this concession doesn't apply to cash loans which can be obtained with this type of credit card.)

Many chain stores issue their own credit or charge cards; some people hold several cards to cover their shopping needs. The method of calculating interest varies from card to card. You should therefore read the terms carefully.

Hire purchase (HP) – as with a credit sale, you pay for the goods by instalments. You own them only when you have paid every instalment. Of course, you mustn't sell the goods until they are legally yours. Once you've paid one-third of the total amount payable the owner (usually a finance company) cannot reclaim the goods without a court order.

Interest is normally at a fixed rate throughout the agreement. It varies from supplier to supplier but can be one of the more expensive ways to borrow.

A consumer who buys a car or motor cycle without knowing it is the subject of an outstanding HP agreement is normally protected. Finance companies have a register of motor vehicles being bought on HP – you can check through a Citizens Advice Bureau (see page 69) or motoring organisation.

Credit sale – offered by shops for the purchase of goods and similar in some ways to hire purchase except that the goods belong to you at once. You normally have to pay a deposit, then weekly/monthly instalments over a fairly short period (usually up to nine months). Interest is at a fixed rate throughout the agreement, but varies slightly from shop to shop. A few stores offer interest-free credit for certain goods, but you may be able to buy the same thing cheaper elsewhere.

Credit unions formed by groups of people with a common bond. Members make regular savings to form a pool of money, from which they can get low cost loans to help with bills, or to pay for clothes, furniture and holidays.

Finance company personal loan – used to pay for a specific and major item, and commonly arranged for you by department stores, car dealers and some electricity and gas boards. You might, however, get a slightly cheaper loan direct from another finance company, so shop around. The minimum you can borrow is around £100 or £200, and you may be asked for security (see 'Mortgage lending'). The repayment period is up to three years. These loans can be expensive, although – to make a sale – car manufacturers sometimes arrange low interest rate loans for buyers.

Mail order credit – offered by the large catalogue companies: their agents may collect your repayments. The credit is often described as 'interest free', but this expression can be used only where all the repayments add up to the cash price.

If you send your repayments by post, make a careful note of these. Sometimes disputes can arise about alleged arrears.

Moneylenders' loans – anyone who calls on you at home offering you a loan without being asked in writing first, or who stops you in the street is committing a criminal offence. Most moneylenders need a licence, so check with your local Trading Standards Department. These loans can be very expensive indeed but moneylenders will often make loans when no-one else will.

Mortgage lending – lending on a first mortgage to buy a property is offered mainly by building societies, banks and insurance companies but a widening group of other financial bodies is now lending to home buyers. Your property acts as the security. It is one of the cheapest ways of borrowing because of the high degree of security and consequent low risks to a lender.

While first mortgages do not generally come under the Consumer Credit Act, a further loan that uses your house as security (called a 'second mortgage') does. They are often advertised by money-lenders as 'secured loans'. This means you give your house as security, not that the loan in itself is protected. If you do not make all the repayments, you could end up losing the roof over your head.

The Act does give you a chance to change your mind, but only for a few days after you get your first copy of the mortgage document.

Pawnbroking – if you pawn anything the pawnbroker must give you a receipt in the proper form headed 'Notice to Debtor'. Read this carefully because it spells out your rights in getting the pawned goods back. It will tell you how to get back the article and also when the pawnbroker is entitled to sell it. If you can't repay what you owe on the agreed date, you will have to pay regular interest to prevent your goods from being sold.

Trading checks and vouchers, provided by specialist companies, can be exchanged for goods (mostly clothing and soft furnishing) in shops which accept them. An agent calls at your home and supplies a 'check' for any amount between £1 and £30. You repay him in weekly instalments, usually over 20 weeks, including a charge for credit outstanding. ('Vouchers' are for larger amounts and repayable over much longer periods.)

Check trading is more common in some parts of the country than others. Although a convenient way of borrowing, it is normally quite expensive.

Hiring goods

The Consumer Credit Act covers most hiring to individuals involving payment of up to £15,000. Unlike hire purchase (see page 76), when you hire – or rent – goods, you do not have the option to buy them. Hiring things that you're not likely to use often (or ever again), such as a cement mixer, can make good financial sense. But think carefully before agreeing to hire anything for a long period. Ask yourself whether you can afford to keep up the payments, and whether it wouldn't be cheaper to buy the goods outright. Find out whether free maintenance or repair is included in the deal – for certain items, such as a TV set, this could be a 'plus' factor for hiring. Almost all hire and rental agreements can be ended by the hirer after 18 months. Some companies have shorter agreements, which may be more appropriate for you.

Signing agreements

Credit and hire agreements covered by the Act are legally binding so it is important to read them carefully and understand thoroughly the terms offered

before signing. **Never sign a blank form!** With all
credit agreements certain information must be given
on the form, (for example, cash price, amount of loan,
interest details, amount and date of each instalment).
When you sign a credit agreement you will get your
own copy. You may be sent further copies in the post.
If you discuss the deal face-to-face with the trader,
and sign the form at home, you then have a few days
cooling-off period in which to change your mind
(details are on the form). If credit or hire agreements
do not conform with the legal requirements they are
enforceable against you only by a court order. But if
you sign any kind of agreement in a shop,
garage or in a finance company office,
there is no cooling-off period.
You cannot change your mind.

Keeping up the payments

If you get into difficulties with the payments, discuss your problem as soon as possible with the shop or finance company. Depending on the type of agreement you have with them, they may allow you a longer time to pay. If they send you a default notice, it must say what the lender intends to do and inform you of your rights under the Act. If your default can be remedied, it must also tell you how it can be straightened out. If you're in doubt, don't hesitate to go to your local consumer adviser for help (see page 69).

Early settlement

Alternatively, you may find you have more money than you expected and want to settle early. In this case the lender will normally have to allow you a rebate of some of the interest originally agreed to cover the whole period of the loan. If, however, you settle fairly early in the life of the agreement, you may well have to pay more than you originally borrowed.

Insurance for loans

Even if insurance is not compulsory by the lender (and lenders sometimes insist you use their insurance), think about taking out insurance against death, sickness or unemployment when you commit yourself to any substantial credit agreement – double glazing or house purchase for example.

Credit licences

Nearly all businesses which offer credit or hire or which are involved with credit in some way (such as debt collectors, and credit reference agencies) must be licensed by the Office of Fair Trading and their names kept on a public register. Only those judged fit to be in a business concerned with credit get licences. Licences can, of course, be taken away. If you feel you have been unfairly treated in a transaction involving credit tell your local Trading Standards Department (see page 68). Apart from the rules governing advertisements and quotations for credit, which help you shop around for the best deal, the Consumer Credit Act and its regulations cover other aspects of credit affecting consumers. Here are some of the more important.

Doorstep credit

Even if traders are licensed under the Act, they must not call uninvited on you at home, nor stop you in the street, to offer cash loans or to put you in touch with someone who can give you a loan. Provided they are licensed to do so however, they may call on you or stop you in the street to sell goods or services available on credit.

It is also illegal for traders to send you a credit card you haven't asked for, or to send anything through the post to people under 18 inviting them to borrow money or obtain other credit facilities.

Brokers' fees

If you have asked a broker to arrange a loan (including a mortgage), he mustn't charge more than £3 for his services if you don't sign an agreement with the potential lender within six months. If you have paid more than £3 in these circumstances, the excess must be returned. If, however, you are seeking a loan of more than £15,000 the broker can also charge you for things like survey fees.

Refused credit?

A trader doesn't have to give you credit or hire out
goods, nor does he have to say why he won't do so.
You have, however, the right to ask for the name and
address of any credit reference agency he may have
consulted about you and to have inaccurate
information held on you by the agency put right.
Your request must be in writing and you must enclose
a non-returnable fee of £1.

Equal liability

Normally, if goods or services bought on credit prove
faulty you are entitled to complain to the seller about
them. But what if the seller has become bankrupt,
gone into liquidation or just refuses to co operate,
leaving you with an expensive item that doesn't work
and you're still paying for?

If any item or service you've bought on credit costs more than £100, and you have a claim against the seller for misrepresentation or breach of contract, you may also have a claim against the credit company which financed the deal and is equally liable. This is a special right given by the Consumer Credit Act.

If you are buying on HP the company providing the credit is in law the seller. So, strictly, it is responsible if there is something wrong with the goods. But, provided the supplier of the goods is still trading, it is best to contact him first. Put everything in writing and always keep copies of letters.

Occasionally the seller of the goods finances credit for you out of his own money, so supplier and seller are one and the same person.

Equal liability doesn't apply where you have been lent money to spend as you wish – that is, where the loan is not tied to the purchase of some specific item or service. So if you get a cash loan from a bank or anywhere else to buy goods or services, there may be no liability on the part of the lender for faulty goods.

Extortionate credit

If you think you're being charged an extortionately high amount for any kind of credit agreement (whenever made), you can say so before a court. If the court agrees, it can help in various ways. For example, it can order the lender to repay unreasonable interest charges. But bear in mind that because certain kinds of credit cost more than others, your view of what is 'extortionate' may not be the court's! Before taking action, consult a consumer adviser (see page 69).

Work out your income

Personal budget

Can you read your meter?

Priority debts

Tell your creditors

Going to court

Getting advice

Keeping out of debt

'I don't know where my money goes.'

If you always seem to be short of money, start
keeping a personal budget. It's a way of working out
how much money you get and how much you spend.

It shows where it goes – on food, bills, clothes or travel. It's useful to list your outgoings and tot them up against your income. It also helps to plan your future spending if you want to start saving for something, like a holiday. Here are some sample charts, but you may need to make changes to suit your circumstances.

Work out your income

Your income	
Type of income	**Amount** (weekly/monthly) £
Wages – your pay	
– overtime	
– your partner's pay	
Social Security Benefits	
Sick benefit	
Family income supplement	
Child benefit	
Unemployment benefit	
Supplementary benefit	
Housing benefit	
Disability benefit	
Maintenance payment	
Retirement pension	
Other Pension	
Any other income .... (eg from lodger)	
TOTAL NET INCOME	£

Personal budget

Now you know how much money you have, work out your outgoings by filling in this chart.

Your personal budget
Fill in this chart to help you sort out your outgoings.

Housing costs	Amount (weekly/monthly) £
Rent/mortgage	
Rates	
Water rates	
House insurance	
Gas	
Electricity	
Coal	
Other fuel	
TOTAL	£
Housekeeping (food, cleaning materials)	
Phone	
TV rental	
TV licence	
Video rental	
Pocket money (children)	
Travel to work	
Car running costs – petrol, oil	
Car insurance	
Newspapers/magazines	
Cigarettes	
Alcohol	
Entertainment: pub, meals out	
cinema, theatre	
sports, clubs	
Clothing	
TOTAL	£

Credit commitments

(1) eg. car ....
(2) washing machine ....
(3) credit card ....
(4) store credit cards ....
(5) ....

TOTAL	£

TOTAL WEEKLY/MONTHLY EXPENDITURE	£

If you're lucky you'll have some money left over. This is your disposable income. But if your outgoings exceed your income you've got a problem! Try cutting down on non-essentials – perhaps cigarettes or eating out, you'll have to decide for yourself.

Work out whether you can increase your income – perhaps by taking a lodger or a part-time job. Check with your local DHSS office or Citizens Advice Bureau to see if you are entitled to any benefits.

'I can't pay my bills. What can I do?'

- Don't panic.

- Don't ignore letters or demands. The longer you leave it, the worse it will get.

- Get in contact with your creditors straight away and explain your present difficulties.

- Don't borrow money to pay off debts without thinking carefully. This could lead you into other problems.

- Always tackle your priority debts first – mortgage/rent, rates, gas, electricity and water (see chart).

If you learn to read your meter, you can keep an eye on how much gas and electricity you are using. You can also check that the reading taken by the board is correct.

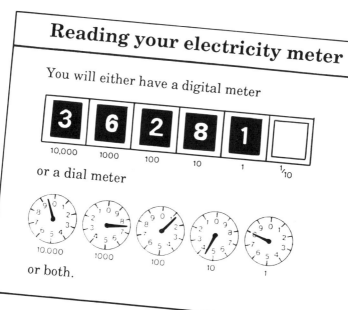

Reading your electricity meter

You will either have a digital meter

or a dial meter

or both.

- Read the black dials only. Ignore the red ones.

- Watch out for the different way each dial goes round.

- Read the numbers on the dial that the hand has just passed.

- When the hand is between two numbers read the lower number.

You read your gas meter in a similar way.

Your debt position		
Priority debts*	**Payment date**	**Arrears** £
1. Rent/Mortgage 2. Gas 3. Electricity 4. Rates 5. Water rates		
	TOTAL	£

Priority debts

These are the type of debts that can cause most trouble. You must always deal with them first. Use any disposable income (money left over) to make arrangements with your creditors, before trying to sort out your other debts.

Act quickly with these priorities — **otherwise** you could:

- lose your home (if you don't pay your rent/ mortgage);

- land up in court (if you don't pay your rate arrears);

- have your fuel/water supply cut off (if you don't pay gas, electricity and water bills).

If you've paid less than one-third off hire purchase goods they could be re-possessed without a court order.

Tell your creditors

If you have a small amount left over or nothing at all when your essential expenses have been paid – tell your creditors immediately. Send them a financial statement (see page 89) to show exactly where your money is going. You can explain what offer you can make to pay off your debt. Aim to show how much you need to live on and that your offer is fair.

List your credit debts to get a clear picture.

Credit commitments*	Payment date	Total amount outstanding
6. Credit card 7. Catalogue 8. Bank loan 9. Other loan 10. HP 11. 12. 13.		
TOTAL		£
TOTAL OF PRIORITY DEBTS PLUS CREDIT COMMITMENTS		£

*These are only examples – you may have others.

You may be tempted to borrow again to get out of debt, but do not do this without getting advice. Rates of interest for this type of borrowing can be high. Adverts do not always make it clear that if you don't pay back on time you can lose your home. A 'secured' loan means the security is your home!

Going to court

Court action is used as a last resort, but don't be frightened. You will be treated fairly and won't land up in jail. You can get advice about the forms and steps involved from a Citizens Advice Bureau or law centre.

- Don't ignore court papers.

- Complete the forms which you get with the summons and send them back to the court as quickly as possible. Get advice if necessary.

- Make sure you attend any court hearings which are arranged.

Getting advice

If your money problems are getting out of hand, seek help. Find out if there is a Money Advice Centre in your area. If not, try a Citizens Advice Bureau. A law centre or legal aid solicitor may also be able to help.

Financial statement

Your name: ....

Your address: ....

....

Weekly/monthly income	Amount £
Net wages	
Total income from benefits	
Other	
TOTAL	£

Essential weekly/monthly spending

Rent/mortgage	
Rates	
Water rates	
House insurance	
Gas	
Electricity	
Other fuel	
Housekeeping	
TV rental	
TV licence	
Travelling expenses	
School meals	
Other	
TOTAL	£
Available disposable income for paying debts **TOTAL**	£
MY CREDITORS ARE: – – – –	
Once priority debts have been agreed, I can offer to pay	£

Eight steps to follow
Freehold and leasehold
Buying a flat
Estate Agents Act 1979
Insuring your home
Buildings insurance
Contents insurance

Buying your home

Buying your own home
is one of the largest purchases
you are likely to make.
If you're unlucky,
the process can be costly,
drawn-out and full of pitfalls.
But it needn't be.
Here are the steps to follow.

Step 1

Decide how much of your own money you can put towards the purchase. Work out how much you want to borrow and can afford to repay each month. Don't forget to allow for the extra running costs you will be taking on – fuel bills, rates and insurance. Remember that you will have to pay solicitor's, surveyor's, Land Registry fees and stamp duty, even before you start thinking about furnishing your new home.

Step 2

Ask a building society, bank or other reputable lender about finance before you start looking. Arrange your mortgage 'in principle' so that everything is ready when you need it.

Step 3

Get estate agents in your chosen area to send you details of the type of property you want. Scan local papers and compare local prices.

Step 4

Once you've found the flat or house you like, make an offer 'subject to contract'.

Step 5

Once your offer is accepted apply formally for a mortgage, arrange for a survey and find a solicitor/ conveyancer to handle the legal paperwork.

Step 6

Before you exchange contracts make sure that your own survey has not revealed any problems.

Step 7

Don't sign the contract until you are certain you will have adequate finance. You must insure the property at the time contracts are being exchanged.

Step 8

Arrange to move in – the property is legally yours on completion day.

In Scotland things are different. Once you make an offer which is accepted, it is binding (neither you nor the seller can change your mind). So you should have a survey done and apply for a mortgage before making your offer.

Freehold and leasehold

Most flats are sold **leasehold** – when your lease expires the flat belong to the land owner. Houses are normally **freehold** – the building and the land on which it stands belong to you. Some houses are, however, sold leasehold but the freehold can be bought after a certain number of years.

Buying a flat

Take care with flats. You need to know how much the **ground rent** is. Find out who is responsible for maintenance and repairs and how these are paid for. Who cleans the hall and stairs? There might be a **service charge**: find out what it is and what it covers. Who insures the building? Get your solicitor to sort out all these matters for you.

Estate Agents Act 1979

The Director General of Fair Trading can ban an estate agent from acting for clients in the buying and selling of property if the agent is found to be 'unfit'. Alternatively the Director General can warn the agent that if he continues to operate in certain undesirable ways, he will be considered unfit and therefore banned.

An estate agent must obey the following rules:

☐ He must tell you beforehand how much his fees are, and when they must be paid.

☐ He must tell you if he has a personal interest in the property you are buying or selling.

☐ If you give the agent a 'contract/pre-contract deposit', he must pay it immediately into a special **client account**. He must keep records which clearly show what he has done with any of your money in that account. In certain cases the agent may have to pay interest on your money while it is in his possession.

Pre-contract deposits are not permitted in Scotland.

Insuring your home

You buy insurance to protect the things you value, such as your home and belongings. Yet most people choose a policy without giving it much thought. You should shop around for an insurance policy that suits you best, just as you would for anything else. Too often people only discover what their policy says when they come to claim – and then it may be too late.

Decide what type of cover you want. If you rent your home then you'll just be concerned about insuring your own possessions, whereas if you're a home owner, you have to think about buildings insurance as well. Do you have an item of particular value to insure? Do you want accidental damage cover?

You can approach insurance companies directly or go through a broker. Ask for quotes, but don't just compare prices – also look carefully at what they cover and what they don't. Study the exclusions. Is there an excess – do you have to pay anything towards the cost of the claim? Does the company have a good reputation for settling claims fast and fairly? Read the policy thoroughly. If you are not sure about something or have a specific query, ask for an explanation.

Buildings insurance covers the building itself including things like built-in kitchen units. Most policies cover damage to your home by fire, explosion, flood or subsidence. There are, however, limits and exceptions to every policy. To find out what **your** policy does or does not cover you'll have to read it!

Contents insurance covers your moveable belongings. There are two types of cover – **indemnity** where a deduction is made for wear and tear, and **new-for-old**, where you receive enough to replace what you have lost with a brand new item. You can buy extra cover to protect your belongings against accidental damage – in case you spill red wine on your cream carpet.

If you have a complaint over an insurance policy see pages 116–117 for advice on what to do.

Codes of practice
Public utilities
Personal finance and insurance
Some other useful bodies

Who cares?

Codes of practice

Many trade associations (and some other bodies) have codes of practice – rules for their members to follow, which should provide a better deal and improved standards of service for customers. To show he supports a code of practice, a trader usually displays the trade association's symbol on his premises. Symbols may also be displayed in adverts, leaflets and brochures.

One advantage of codes of practice is that traders are expected to observe them in spirit as well as to the letter. Codes can therefore contain provisions which couldn't easily be covered by law (such as a promise to deal with complaints promptly and politely). They can be tailored to the particular circumstances of each trade or industry, and be adjusted as needs arise. By contrast, changing the law is time-consuming and expensive, and puts an extra burden on those who have to enforce it.

Codes include such points as: better pre-shopping information; improved standards in the supply of goods or services; clear price displays; realistic estimates for delivery of goods or completion of repairs; prompt and helpful servicing arrangements; prohibitions on unfair or misleading trade practices; and staff training. All codes have conciliation schemes for investigating disputes which cannot be sorted out between traders and customers themselves. Some also have an independent arbitration scheme – not to be confused with the simplified system for settling small claims in the county courts of England and Wales and Northern Ireland, which is also referred to as arbitration (see page 64).

If you can't sort out your complaint by going back to the shop or getting in touch with the manufacturer, it's worth finding out if there is a trade association which can help. Listed on the following pages are some of the organisations – mainly trade associations – which have codes of practice.

Advertising

Advertising Standards Authority
Brook House, 2–16 Torrington Place, London WC1E 7HN
Telephone: 01–580 5555

The ASA is an independent body which administers two codes:

The British Code of Advertising Practice covers most forms of
advertising in the media and in cinemas, but not on TV or radio.
The code is intended to ensure that adverts are legal, decent,
honest and truthful. It also has detailed rules on advertising dealing
with such matters as slimming, medicinal and health products,
alcohol, smoking, finance, mail order and testimonials. Complaints
made to the ASA are investigated and, if necessary, taken up with
the advertiser. A copy of the offending advert should be enclosed
with any complaint.

The British Code of Sales Promotion Practice covers competitions,
the use of children in promotions, and the quality, value and
suitability of goods offered (for example, as 'free gifts', prizes, or
'reduced-price offers'). The complaints system is the same as for
advertising.

Independent Broadcasting Authority
70 Brompton Road, London SW3 1EY
Telephone: 01–584 7011

The IBA Code of Advertising Standards and Practice covers all
television, independent radio and ORACLE teletext advertisements.
Among other things, it says they should not play on fear or
superstition, nor be excessively noisy. Any price comparisons made
must be accurate and not misleading.

The code pays particular attention to medicinal and health products,
alcohol and financial advertising and to references to guarantees
and testimonials. Special rules apply to child audiences and the use
of children in adverts.

Securities and Investments Board
3 Royal Exchange Buildings, Cornhill, London EC3V 3NL
Telephone: 01–283 2474

The SIB is responsible for advertising by persons authorised to carry
on investment business under the Financial Services Act 1986.

Cars and motorcycles

Motor Agents' Association Ltd
National Conciliation Service,
73 Park Street, Bristol BS1 5PS
Telephone: Bristol (0272) 293232

**Society of Motor Manufacturers
and Traders Ltd**
Forbes House, Halkin Street,
London SW1X 7DS
Telephone: 01–235 7000

Scottish Motor Trade Association Ltd
Customer Complaints Service,
3 Palmerston Place, Edinburgh EH12 5AQ
Telephone: 031–225 3643

Vehicle Builders and Repairers Association
Belmont House, Gildersome, Leeds LS27 7TW
Telephone: Leeds (0532) 538333

All the motor trade associations follow codes which offer
conciliation and arbitration services for disputes involving members.
The Motor Agents Association and Scottish Motor Trade Association
also deal with complaints made about motorcycles purchased
through their members.

Caravans

**The British Holiday and
Home Parks Association Ltd**
Chichester House, 31 Park Road,
Gloucester GL1 1LH
Telephone: Gloucester (0452) 26911

The National Caravan Council
Catherine House, Victoria Road, Aldershot,
Hants GU11 1SS
Telephone: Aldershot (0252) 318251

The two holiday caravan codes offer protection to consumers hiring
or owning holiday caravans. The codes set out conditions that park
owners must meet.

Consumer credit

Finance Houses Association Ltd
18 Upper Grosvenor Street, London W1X 9PB
Telephone: 01–491 2783

Consumer Credit Trade Association
Tennyson House, 159–163 Great Portland Street,
London W1N 5FD
Telephone: 01–636 7564

National Consumer Credit Association (UK) Ltd
Queen's House, Queen's Road, Chester CH1 3BQ
Telephone: Chester (0244) 312044

National Consumer Credit Federation
98–100 Holme Lane, Sheffield S6 4JW
Telephone: Sheffield (0742) 348101

The four associations which, between them, represent a large
proportion of those companies that handle consumer credit business
have all adopted codes of practice. Although they differ in detail, all
the codes contain important provisions intended to prevent
consumers being pressurised into accepting credit, to ensure that
they are not granted credit beyond their means to repay. They also
provide for arbitration to settle disputes.

Direct selling

Direct Selling Association Ltd
44 Russell Square, London WC1B 4JP
Telephone: 01–580 8433

'Direct selling' covers goods sold at organised parties in private
homes, and goods sold at the door.

The DSA code requires hostesses to make clear to guests the
purpose of a party. Customers have 14 days in which to change
their minds about goods ordered and get their deposits back. All
sales leaflets must show the company's name and address.

For doorstep sales, the code requires representatives to carry
identification cards and to carry company literature on the products/
services offered. Customers also have 14 days to cancel agreements
and claim full refunds on deposits. The DSA offers informal
conciliation on disputes.

Double glazing

Glass and Glazing Federation
44–48 Borough High Street, London SE1 1XB
Telephone: 01–403 7177

The GGF code covers all members' business with consumers, whether direct or through retail outlets, from the initial promotion to after-sales service. Features include: contracts which set out the procedure to be followed when work is not completed on time; a scheme to protect deposits; and a conciliation and arbitration scheme.

The GGF abides by Office of Fair Trading guidelines in the use of the telephone in both selling products and in making appointments.

Electrical goods

Association of Manufacturers of Domestic Electrical Appliances
Leicester House, 8 Leicester Street, London WC2H 7BN
Telephone: 01–437 0678

Most British manufacturers of domestic electrical appliances are members of AMDEA. The AMDEA code covers repairs or servicing done by them or their service agents. It sets out standards for speed and quality of service, guarantees on paid-for repairs, and how long members should stock spare parts. There are conciliation and arbitration schemes to settle disputes.

The Electricity Council (on behalf of the Area Electricity Boards and Consultative Councils in England and Wales), and the Scottish Electricity Boards (together with the Scottish Electricity Consultative Councils) operate similar codes that cover goods serviced or repaired through Electricity Board shops (see under 'Public utilities', on page 112).

**Radio, Electrical and
Television Retailers' Association**
Retra House, 57–61 Newington Causeway,
London SE1 6BE
Telephone: 01–403 1463

The RETRA code lays down standards for the sale and servicing of electrical and electronic goods. The Association has a Customer Conciliation Panel.

Footwear

Footwear Distributors' Federation

Commonwealth House,
1–19 New Oxford Street,
London WC1A 1PA
Telephone: 01–404 0955

Most shoe retailers which belong to the Footwear Distributors' Federation, backed by several other associations, follow the Code of Practice for Footwear. The code says that members offer advice and information about materials used in the shoes you buy. If something does go wrong, the shop should deal with your complaints promptly. Shoes can be independently tested at the Footwear Testing Centre, and the shop must abide by the Centre's decision. There is a small fee to pay, but this is refundable if the report is in your favour.

Funerals

National Association of Funeral Directors

57 Doughty Street, London WC1N 2NE
Telephone: 01–242 9388

The NAFD code requires members to provide a simple, basic funeral at an inclusive price; written estimates with detailed charges; and guidance on how to deal with death certificates. NAFD runs a conciliation service and there is independent arbitration to settle disputes.

Services provided by florists and gravestone suppliers are not covered.

Furniture

National Association of Retail Furnishers

17–21 George Street, Croydon, Surrey CR9 1TQ
Telephone : 01–680 8444

The Furniture Code of Practice is supported by five associations (including manufacturers). NARF will try to settle disputes about furniture bought in its members' shops, sometimes using an inspection service.

Under the code, furniture should have labels attached if information is not otherwise readily available, giving pre-shopping advice such as dimensions, construction details, care and cleaning instructions.

Laundries and dry cleaning

**Association of British Laundry Cleaning
and Rental Services Ltd**
7 Churchill Court, 58 Station Road,
North Harrow, Middx HA2 7SA
Telephone: 01–863 7755

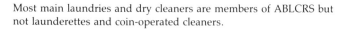

Most main laundries and dry cleaners are members of ABLCRS but
not launderettes and coin-operated cleaners.

The ABLCRS code covers all services normally provided, including
repairs and dyeing. Through its Customer Advisory Service,
ABLCRS deals with queries and complaints about member firms. If
necessary, the Advisory Service can arrange laboratory test facilities.

Mail order

**Mail Order Traders Association
of Great Britain**
25 Castle Street, Liverpool L2 4TD
Telephone: 051–227 4181

All the large catalogue companies are members of MOTA. The
MOTA code provides for prompt delivery dates; the return of
unwanted or faulty goods; servicing arrangements; and a
complaints procedure. Complain in writing and quote your
reference number.

Mail Order Publishers' Authority
1 New Burlington Street, London W1X 1FD
Telephone: 01–437 0706

Members of the Association of Mail Order Publishers are firms
which publish books, magazines or records sold by post. Their code
covers the way goods are advertised and conditions about despatch.
Members must review their debt-collection methods and ensure that
customers are not bothered without good reason. The Authority
will try to settle unresolved disputes.

Newspaper mail order protection schemes

Most newspapers, magazines and periodicals belong to associations
which have mail order protection schemes. Under these schemes,
you are protected if you send off money for goods to an advertiser
who goes into liquidation or bankruptcy before he sends those

goods. Provided you apply to the Advertisement Manager of the publication which carried the advertisement, within the time specified, you should get your money back. (All publications which support a scheme carry details about how to claim.) The Advertisement Manager may also investigate complaints about late deliveries, refunds, faulty goods and the way goods are advertised.

The schemes do not cover classified advertisements or traders who advertise catalogues from which you have to order goods.

British Code of Advertising Practice

The advertising practice code of the Advertising Standards Authority (see page 105) requires mail order traders to deliver goods (except plants and made-to-measure items) within 28 days, or to tell you if they cannot. They must also promptly refund your money if you return unwanted goods undamaged within seven days, or if your goods are not delivered within 28 days and you decide you no longer want them.

Both the mail order trade associations shown require their members to abide by the advertising practice code.

Motorcycles

The Code of Practice for the Motorcycle Industry is supported by the Motor Cycle Association of Great Britain Ltd and the Motorcycle Retailers Association (a subsidiary of the Motor Agents Association). Complaints are handled by the Motor Agents Association or the Scottish Motor Trade Association (see page 106).

Photography

— representing film and equipment manufacturers

British Photographic Association
Carolyn House, 22–26 Dingwall Road, Croydon, Surrey CR0 9XF
Telephone: 01–688 4422

— representing retail pharmacists

National Pharmaceutical Association
Mallinson House, 40–42 St Peter's Street, St Albans, Herts AL1 3NP
Telephone: St Albans (0727) 32161

— representing film processors

Association of Photographic Laboratories
9 Warwick Court, Grays Inn,
London WC1R 5DJ
Telephone: 01–405 2762/4253

— representing repairers

**Institute of Photographic Apparatus
Repair Technicians**
228 Regent's Park Road, Finchley,
London N3 3HP
Telephone: 01–346 8302

We honour
the Code of Practice
for the
Photographic Industry

Prepared in consultation with the Office of Fair Trading

The Code of Practice for the Photographic Industry is supported by
10 associations. It covers cameras, equipment, repairs, film
developing and professional photography. Unresolved complaints
are dealt with by the associations shown.

Travel

Association of British Travel Agents
55–57 Newman Street, London W1P 4AH
Telephone: 01–637 2444

ABTA

ABTA represents most well-known tour operators and travel agents.

The ABTA code covers booking conditions, insurance cover,
cancellations, alterations, surcharges, overbooking, and complaints
about package holidays. ABTA operates a central fund to help
safeguard your money if a member firm collapses or defaults. There
is a conciliation service and an independent arbitration scheme.

There are Tourist Boards for England, Scotland, Wales and
Northern Ireland which can assist with complaints about holiday
services and facilities in the United Kingdom. You can get addresses
from local tourist information centres and local consumer advisers.

Public utilities

Such services as gas, electricity, post and telephones, British Rail,
and other public utilities usually have a Consumer or Consultative
Council to help sort out problems.

First, try to sort the matter out with the people on the spot. Look in the local phone book under 'Gas', 'Electricity', 'Post Office', etc and find the department you need – 'Accounts', 'Sales', 'Servicing' or simply 'Customer Enquiries'. Or look on the back of your latest bill which usually has the main contact points. Explain your problem. Then, if you still don't get satisfaction, contact the appropriate consumer body.

Airlines

Air Transport Users' Committee
129 Kingsway, London WC2B 6NN
Telephone: 01–242 3882

The committee can look into complaints against any airline, not just British ones.

Airport facilities

Within the United Kingdom most major airports have an Airport Consultative Committee; at smaller airports complaints should be made to the airport manager.

Bus services

Contact the Local Traffic Commissioner (address from your local council offices). In London contact:

London Regional Passengers' Committee
Golden Cross House, 8 Duncannon Street, London WC2N 4JF
Telephone: 01–839 1898/9

British Rail

There is a Code of Practice for Passenger Travel. Copies are available at main stations. It explains how to deal with ticket refunds and losses, how to make complaints and how to claim compensation. There is also an independent arbitration scheme.

If your problem cannot be solved on the spot, contact the local Area Manager. The problem can also be referred to the Secretary of the local Transport Users' Consultative Committee (address from railway stations or the phone book). In London, contact the London Regional Passengers' Committee (address under 'Bus services').

Coal and other solid fuels

The coal industry operates the Approved Coal Merchants' Scheme.
If you have a complaint which you cannot resolve with your coal
merchant, contact the Scheme's area secretary. If you still have no
success seek advice from:

Domestic Coal Consumers' Council
Gaverelle House, 2 Bunhill Row, London EC1Y 8LL
Telephone: 01-638 8914

Electricity

Contact the Electricity Consultative Council for your area (address
from your bill, showroom or the phone book). In Northern Ireland,
contact the General Consumer Council for Northern Ireland.

Gas

Contact the regional office for your area of the Gas Consumers'
Council (address from your bill, showroom or the phone book), or:

OFGAS (Office of Gas Supply)
Southside, 105 Victoria Street, London SW1E 6QT
Telephone: 01–828 0898

Postal services

There is a code of practice covering postal services. Any complaints
should be made first to your local post office. Where they exist you
can approach your local Post Office Advisory Committee (POAC) –
the address is in your phone book. If you still have no success, or if
there is no POAC in your area, contact:

Post Office Users' National Council (POUNC)
Waterloo Bridge House, Waterloo Road, London SE1 8UA
Telephone: 01–928 9458

(There are separate offices in Scotland, Wales and Northern Ireland
– see the phone book for details. They will investigate complaints.)

Telephones

The British Telecom Code of Practice for Consumers is set out in
your phone book. If you want to complain about an extortionate
phone bill or other British Telecom services, you should first contact
your area office (address on your phone bill), then the local

Telecommunications Advice Committee (TAC), if there is one. (Its address is in the phone book.) You can also get advice from the Secretary of the appropriate national Advisory Committee on Telecommunications (the addresses are at the back of your phone book.) If necessary they will consult the Office of Telecommunications (OFTEL). You can also contact OFTEL direct at:

Office of Telecommunications
Atlantic House, Holborn Viaduct, London EC1N 2HQ
Telephone: 01–822 1650 (for consumer complaints)

Water

Contact your local Water Consumer Consultative Committee (address from your Water Authority). In Scotland, contact the Water Services Department for your Region. In Northern Ireland, contact the Water Services Department at the Department of the Environment for Northern Ireland for the region in which you live.

Personal finance and insurance

Banks

Office of the Banking Ombudsman,
Citadel House, 5–11 Fetter Lane, London EC4A 1BR
Telephone: 01–583 1395

If you have tried to sort out your problem with your local branch manager and the head office with no success, the Ombudsman may be able to help you.

Building societies

The Office of the Building Societies' Ombudsman
Grosvenor Gardens House, 35–37 Grosvenor Gardens, London SW1X 7AW.
Telephone: 01–931 0044

If you think you have suffered financial loss, expense or inconvenience as a result of unfair treatment or maladministration by your building society – and you cannot resolve the matter with the society itself – contact the Ombudsman, who will consider your complaint.

Insurance brokers

The Financial Intermediaries, Managers and Brokers Regulatory Association
22 Great Tower Street, London EC3R 5AQ
Telephone: 01–929 2711

Deals with complaints under the Financial Services Act 1986, about independent intermediaries who sell or advise on unit trusts, life assurance and other investments.

The Insurance Brokers Registration Council
15 St Helens Place, London EC3A 6DS
Telephone: 01–588 4387

Deals with complaints concerning unprofessional conduct of an insurance broker registered under the Insurance Brokers (Registration) Act 1977.

British Insurance and Investment Brokers' Association
BIIBA House, 14 Bevis Marks, London EC3A 7NT
Telephone: 01–623 9043

Deals with complaints and enquiries relating to the part played by a broker, as opposed to an insurance company if the broker is a member.

Life and non-life insurance

Insurance Ombudsman Bureau
31 Southampton Row, London WC1B 5HJ
Telephone: 01–242 8613

If you cannot resolve your problem by talking to the company write with your complaint, giving the name of the company and your policy number.

Personal Insurance Arbitration Service
Chartered Institute of Arbitrators, International Arbitration Centre, 75 Cannon Street, London EC4N 5BH
Telephone: 01–236 8761

Provides for the settlement of disputes with a number of insurance companies.

Lloyd's
The Manager – Customer Enquiries
London House, 6 London Street, London EC3R 7AB
Telephone: 01–623 7100

Deals with complaints about Lloyd's insurance when you cannot
obtain satisfaction from the broker concerned.

The Life Assurance and Unit Trust Regulatory Organisation
Centre Point, 103 New Oxford Street, London WC1A 1QH
Telephone: 01–379 0444

Deals with complaints about life assurance and unit trust companies
under the Financial Services Act 1986.

Association of British Insurers
Aldermary House, Queen Street, London EC4N 1TT
Telephone: 01–248 4477

Deals with complaints relating to all types of insurance policies
issued by one of its members.

Friendly societies

The Registry of Friendly Societies
15–17 Great Marlborough Street, London W1V 2AX
Telephone: 01–437 9992

Deals with complaints about policies issued by friendly societies.

'Doorstep' life assurance

Industrial Assurance Commissioner
15 Great Marlborough Street, London W1V 2AZ
Telephone: 01–437 9992

Life assurance policies on which premiums are collected by agents
at policyholder's homes at intervals of less than two months come
within the official jurisdiction of the Commissioner.

The **Commissioner for Northern Ireland** has his office at:

64 Chichester Street, Belfast BT1 4JX
Telephone: Belfast (0232) 234488

Solicitors
Solicitors Complaints Bureau
Portland House, Stag Place, London SW1E 5BL
Telephone: 01–834 2288

Handles complaints against solicitors, such as inefficiency, overcharging, delays in dealing with your case.

Note: The Bureau covers England and Wales only.

Anti-discrimination bodies
Commission for Racial Equality
Elliot House, Allington Street, London SW1 5EH
Telephone: 01–828 7022

Equal Opportunities Commission
Overseas House, Quay Street, Manchester M3 3HN
Telephone: 061–833 9244

Discrimination in the supply of goods and services on the grounds of race or sex is forbidden by law. The Commissions were set up to help enforce the law. If you have reason to think a trader has discriminated against you, ask your local Citizens Advice Bureau how you can take the matter further. Or write directly to the appropriate Commission.

Hearing aids
Hearing Aid Council
1st Floor, Ashton House, 471 Silvery Boulevard, Milton Keynes MK9 2LP
Telephone: Milton Keynes (0908) 585442

BEAB Marks

BSI marks

National Inspection Council for Electrical
Installation Contracting

Confederation for the Registration of
Gas Installers

Home Laundering Consultative Council

Furniture safety

Look out for labels

Here are a few labels you will see in shops giving advice, information or warning.

BEAB marks

Equipment bearing any of these three marks has been approved by the British Electrotechnical Approvals Board. The marks must be prominently displayed on or near the rating plate and may also be found on swing labels attached to the equipment.

Mark A –
the Mark of Safety appears only on electric blankets. It means that samples of the blanket have been tested to comply with certain standards.

Mark B –
means a sample of the product will have been tested to a regulated standard.

Mark C –
shows that a sample of the product has been tested and approved by another European Approvals Authority to a standard broadly equivalent to the British Standard.

BSI marks

The Kitemark
This appears on a wide range of products complying with standards laid down by the British Standards Institution – from car safety belts to pressure cookers.

The safety mark

This appears only on goods which comply with British Standards of Safety – like certain types of gas appliances and light fittings.

Manufacturers wishing to use either of the above marks must first submit their products to BSI for testing. Periodic tests of the goods and factory are carried out.

The BSI has a Consumer Policy Committee at 2 Park Street, London W1A 2BS.

National Inspection Council for Electrical Installation Contracting

Your local Electricity Board shop has a list of reliable contractors in your area, who may display this label. These contractors are regularly inspected and approved by the National Inspection Council for Electrical Installation Contracting, an independent non-profit-making organisation set up to protect the interests of electricity consumers against faulty, unsafe, or otherwise defective workmanship.

APPROVED CONTRACTOR

Confederation for the Registration of Gas Installers

Your local British Gas showroom has a list of installers registered with the Confederation for the Registration of Gas Installers. The work of CORGI registered installers is regularly checked to ensure that it is up to standard and complies with Gas Safety Regulations.

Home Laundering Consultative Council

Look for the International Textile Care labels on clothes giving the recommendations about washing, bleaching, tumble drying, ironing and dry-cleaning. Each of the five symbols represents a specific instruction. A Textile Care Labelling Symbols Guide is available from HLCC at the British Apparel Centre, 7 Swallow Place, London W1R 7AA.

Furniture safety

This label means that the furniture satisfies only the minimum requirement under the regulations for resistance to smouldering cigarettes. The furniture must also carry a permanent label warning that careless use of matches can set fire to it.

This label means that the furniture has passed the tests for resistance to both cigarettes and matches.

Note: New legal requirements are under consideration.

Consumers' Association Ltd
National Consumer Council
National Federation of Consumer Groups

Consumer bodies ▯

Consumers' Association Ltd
2 Marylebone Road, London NW1 4DX
Telephone: 01–486 5544

The Association for Consumer Research (ACR) is a registered
charity which carries out research and comparative testing of goods
and services. Its trading subsidiary Consumers' Association Ltd
(CA) publishes the research and results in the monthly magazine
Which? CA also publishes books on many consumer topics. Which?
Personal Service gives legal advice to subscribers.

National Consumer Council
20 Grosvenor Gardens, London SW1W 0DH
Telephone: 01–730 3469

The Council was established by the Government in 1975. It watches
over consumers' interests and speaks up for the consumer to
Government, nationalised industries, commerce, and public and
private services. It has no statutory powers but carries out a wide
range of research and publishes its recommendations. There are
Councils for Northern Ireland, Scotland and Wales, and all four
work closely together.

National Federation of Consumer Groups
12 Mosley Street, Newcastle upon Tyne NE1 1DE
Telephone: Tyneside (091) 261 8259

The Federation is the central organisation for voluntary local
consumer groups. It can put you in touch with your local group or
help you to start one. Or you can join the Federation as an
individual member. Groups survey local goods and services,
publish their reports, and campaign for improvements where
necessary. (All enquiries should be accompanied by a stamped
self-addressed envelope.)

Useful Office of Fair Trading publications

Leaflets

How to put things right explains shoppers' legal rights on faulty goods and services (in England and Wales), and where to get help and advice.

Dear shopper in Scotland describes shoppers' rights under Scottish law.

Dear shopper in Northern Ireland tells Northern Ireland consumers about their legal rights.

Don't wave your money goodbye warns of the risks of paying in advance for goods and services, and suggests ways of protecting prepayments.

How to cope with doorstep salesmen highlights some of the selling methods used, and how to deal with problems.

Shop around for credit – a guide to different types of credit, and how to use it wisely.

No credit? explains consumers' rights to know what credit reference agencies say about them.

Debt – a survival guide – a guide to coping with debt.

Home sweet home – a guide for the first-time buyer which looks at some of the problems that can crop up. (There is a Scottish version as well.)

It might never happen but . . . a guide on how to get adequate insurance for homes and personal possessions.

Home improvements warns of the problems that can arise when you employ someone to undertake home improvement work, and what to do if things go wrong.

I'm going to take it further!
Outlines how consumers who are dissatisfied with the initial response to a complaint can seek redress under code arbitration or by going to court.

Office of Fair Trading

Debt

A survival guide

a 6 step ACTION PLAN
a personal budget chart
a financial statement for your creditors

All these publications are free. They are available from local consumer advisers, Trading Standards Departments and many public libraries.

Printed in the United Kingdom for Her Majesty's Stationery Office
Dd 289719 C1000 9/88